Transportation Investment Planning

Transportation Investment Planning

**An Introduction for
Engineers and Planners**

Martin Wohl
Carnegie-Mellon University

Lexington Books
D.C. Heath and Company
Lexington, Massachusetts
Toronto   London

Contents

List of Figures

List of Tables

Acknowledgments

To many colleagues and friends from whom I learned much, and from whom I gained the intellectual stimulation and encouragement to sharpen my interest in the professional areas covered herein, I extend my warmest gratitude. I especially want to thank L.M.K. Boelter (the late Dean of Engineering, U.C.L.A.), A. Scheffer Lang (Professor of Civil Engineering, M.I.T.), Gerald Kraft (President, Charles River Associates, Inc.), Julius Margolis (Professor of Economics, University of Pennsylvania), and John R. Meyer (President, National Bureau of Economic Research).

Despite their aid, I must accept full responsibility for any errors of judgment or fact.

**Transportation Investment
Planning**

1

The Transportation
Investment Problem

The transportation investment problem of public agencies is not simply one of justifying investments or one of minimizing total transport costs. Nor is it one of undertaking the necessary investment to meet some arbitrarily established goal or standard; that is, it is not a problem of building enough facilities to provide every citizen comfortable and convenient access, or one of eliminating congestion or significantly reducing fatal accidents—regardless of all else.

Rather, the problem faced by public transport agencies is one of deciding how best to employ the available technological, material, and human resources for the purpose of providing transportation service, and it is one of determining the appropriate role of the public sector. Implicit are questions of how many resources should be employed, how should they be combined, how should they be utilized, and when (and by whom) should the resources be committed. Involved are both technical and ethical considerations, both human and physical aspects, and both present and future concerns.

The purpose of this book is to provide a framework for analyzing transport investment by public agencies. The analysis will attempt to establish the technical, economic, and social aspects which impinge on the investment problem, to characterize their interrelationship and to provide a foundation for interrelating the technical and ethical considerations, the human and physical aspects, and present and future concerns such that rational public investment decisions can be the practical result, at least in approximate terms. More specifically, the framework and analysis will be detailed for investment in public transport facilities which (principally) serve intercity or through passenger trip movements. Even though attention will primarily be focused on the problem of public investment in and utilization of the supporting way or highways for through trips, the analysis will consider and account for the interactions among all components of the overall highway-vehicle-driver system, will account for all costs—public or private—stemming from the construction, operation, or usage of public ways, and will generally apply to other modal systems.

1.1 General Aspects of the Public Transport
Investment Problem

From an engineering and planning standpoint, the first (and perhaps foremost) consideration rests with the technological devices or facilities which are *or* will be available to provide for passenger (or goods) movement, and with the

1

different ways of using technology or combining the public resources to provide for varying levels of tripmaking volume or service.[a] More simply, in the first instance we must be concerned with the different means and possibilities for providing transportation at different levels of capacity and service,[b] and with the material and labor inputs or requirements associated with these physical possibilities or alternatives. The material and labor inputs or requirements stemming from the different transport alternatives will determine the cost of providing transportation of that capacity and service level, once the prices of acquiring the material and labor items are specified. *Furthermore, in this analysis of public transport investment, the personal resources (time, effort, inconvenience, etc.) committed by the travelers in the process of tripmaking will be regarded as part of the overall transportation costs*; in essence, the inclusion of the personal travel time and effort "costs" within the structure of total transportation costs permits us to account for the service dimension within cost functions and in turn simplifies the dimensional structure of demand functions.[1]

A second concern of the planner and engineer must be with matters of travel demand; that is, with a determination of the volume which *will* use facilities of different capacity or service. Simply, this is a travel forecasting problem and one of determining, on the one hand, how travelers or shippers will perceive the service to be afforded by facilities and, on the other, how many of them will desire to travel under the perceived circumstances of service. As will be shown, this aspect can be resolved only by considering the interaction among the physical system or facility characteristics, the way in which travelers perceive the transport service, and the numbers of travelers which will find travel worthwhile at different levels of service.[c]

A separate but related problem is that of establishing the value or benefit associated with the tripmaking which will be experienced for facilities of varying capacity or service. Distinctions must be made between benefit which *is* received or accrued by travelers, and the relationships between benefit and the factors of demand, transport facility capacity, service and pricing policies must be established and accounted for.

Furthermore, and as a practical matter, engineers and planners will generally find it necessary to focus attention on matters involving the incidence of cost and benefit—that is, on who pays the costs and who accrues the benefits under various investment and pricing policies. As a consequence, it will be necessary to investigate the mechanisms and devices which may be utilized for assessing and recovering costs, and for controlling usage, and to note the way in which efficiency and incidence are affected.

---

[a]"Technology" is used broadly herein, in the sense of all natural or manufactured resources and materials, and any associated labor requirements, which can be used for the construction and operation of physical transport facilities and vehicles operating thereon.

[b]By service, I refer to the level of comfort, convenience, travel speed, privacy, safety, and general mobility afforded the people or goods transported.

[c]Also, tripmaking is functionally related to a host of other activities and opportunities, all of which will be ignored at this stage for simplicity.

The crux of the long-run investment problem is to properly interrelate these aspects and considerations, both within specific time periods (or intratemporally such as hour to hour and day to day during some given year) and between different time periods (or intertemporally such as year to year), to place the benefits and costs on commensurate time and value scales, to characterize the changes in net benefit (or changes in the difference between total benefit and total cost) which stem from various investment, pricing, operational, and staging alternatives, and, on the basis of these data, to determine how best to allocate resources. In so doing, however, some care will be taken to distinguish between the aggregative and differential effects and between the efficiency and distribution effects of various alternatives; in the terms of the economist, "Efficiency questions relate to the size of the pie available; distribution questions, to who gets what share."[2] While the incidence and distributional types of effects are not entirely amenable to precise analysis, and involve a range of ethical considerations, they nevertheless can affect decision-making and investment policy in important ways; thus, at least a cursory investigation of the interactions is desirable if not necessary.

1.2 Some Important Distinctions and Assumptions Regarding the Underlying Market and Social Conditions

Foremost, this book is intended to provide a more formal structure to aid the engineer and planner in his search for and design of "useful and worthwhile devices and facilities." While the engineer only needs a firm knowledge of the technological devices, processes, methods, and techniques in order *to propose and describe* alternative *physical* systems or operations, it should be evident that he can make no judgments about their usefulness or worthwhileness without intensive consideration of the economic consequences. That is, the engineer must consider the interaction of the technology with its economic and social environment; he must evaluate the market for technological alternatives, their expected usage, and the resources commitments and benefits stemming from his proposals.

To pinpoint where the engineering ends and the economics begins is of no importance; but to understand the interplay among the technological, economic, and social considerations is crucial to the engineer's task of designing technologies that are "useful and worthwhile." It is this interplay, as well as an understanding of the underlying structure of economics and of the way in which physical designs are or can be affected by economic considerations, that is the subject of this book. The importance of this broader understanding is more evident when one considers that the key administrators in the government agencies which plan, construct, and operate transport facilities are often engineers and that these men are called upon to employ far more than technological standards for their decision-making.

To date, the formal involvement of the engineer in economic matters has been limited for the most part to economic justification procedures (and, on a more limited basis, matters of capital budgeting).[3] Broader questions of economic efficiency, of investment and pricing policy as they relate to system expansion and operation, and to demand considerations, have by and large gone unnoticed within the engineering community, regardless of the important way in which the "best" or "optimum" technology impinges on such matters.[d] While economic justification and long-run investment principles are directly related and consistent, one with the other, it should be noted that, as normally applied, economic analysis merely permits determination of the "best" economically feasible alternative among a *subset* of proposals, and does not necessarily face the problem of determining the long-run "optimum" among the *entire set* of expansion (or contraction) and operation proposals.

The procedures, principles, and analysis to be discussed herein will generally be restricted in several important (and somewhat unrealistic) respects. The principal ones are: (1) partial, rather general equilibrium analyses will be made; that is, it will be assumed that the commitment of resources to the transport sector will not affect prices for the remainder of the economy or have feedback effects upon the transport demands or upon the costs of supplying transport services;[e] (2) static rather than dynamic analyses will be employed in determining certain interactions between the transport system and the travel demand market; more specifically, certain cross-relations between modes and between hours of travel will be ignored; (3) travelers are assumed to be homogeneous with respect to travel and congestion effects and costs (though not with respect to trip value or utility); that is, it will be assumed that all persons traveling during the same time period (or, say, hour) will suffer the same amount of delay, discomfort, etc., and that all these travelers value the discomfort, delay, and inconvenience incurred equally;[4] and (4) the marginal utility of income will be assumed to be equal for all travelers; that is, the utility of an extra dollar for a poor traveler will be assumed to be equal to that for a well-to-do traveler.

Additional comments are in order with respect to the third assumption, the one regarding homogeneous travel and congestion costs. First, the important distinction must be made between the travel costs and travel value; the former refers to the "expenditures" in time, effort, or money which are made or incurred by the traveler in the course of making a specific trip, while the latter refers to the gross value or, say, satisfaction which the traveler will receive by virtue of making the trip (and *before* deducting or netting out the travel cost). This formulation, while somewhat different from that usually found in micro-

---

[d]This is not to overlook the early and significant work of Jules Dupuit, a French public works engineer.

[e]The assumption is probably insignificant for marginal or incremental improvements and for year to year changes, but for large-scale improvements (e.g., the Interstate highway program), some feedback effects could be anticipated.

economic theory, is consistent with that commonly set forth by transportation economists.[5] Second, there can be no doubt but that the assumption of homogeneous costs is invalid and that different people will be affected by time, effort, and money "expenditures" (and changes in these items) in different ways and to different degrees. However, to properly characterize all of the diverse effects would require multidimensional and interacting cost and demand functions, and would necessitate use of fully dynamic analytical procedures, and of data which almost certainly would extend far beyond our present and foreseeable capabilities. In short, "this assumption of homogeneity is 'unrealistic,' but it does simplify enormously the theoretical development and the empirical tests."[6]

The distortions that result from the four major simplifying assumptions (and others yet to be discussed) cannot presently be fully documented, at least not with any degree of reliability. Simply, the public and private economy cannot be simulated sufficiently to measure the effects on efficiency and distribution of oversimplification. In spite of this, it *seems* desirable to attempt to model the transport system, at least in terms of its more dominant or obvious variables, and to hypothesize the effects of simplification. Also, to the extent possible, the consequences resulting from these assumptions will be recounted in later chapters.

1.3 What Point of View, or "Worthwhile" to Whom?

While the engineering literature often suggests that the techniques for making an appropriate choice among alternative projects are straightforward and simple, it is important to recognize that such is hardly the case. In fact, even to establish the basis for evaluating alternatives—that is, to state what is meant by "worthwhile" and "best," and what factors and elements one includes or excludes—is a most complex and sometimes judgmental procedure.

In deciding whether or not to make specific purchases, individuals continually are evaluating and weighing the alternatives, and are called upon to decide whether it is worthwhile to use their (limited) available funds and resources in one way or another, or to withhold their use until some future time. Presumably, in making each decision, the individual allocates his total resources in a fashion most "worthwhile" *to him.* On a larger scale, a private industrial firm operates in a similar fashion, but considers each alternative use of its resources from *its own* "point of view" or in terms of the most "worthwhile" or profitable investment *to its owners* (or to those whose funds or resources are being risked).

As the individual or group of individuals making investment changes, a shift in "point of view" is generally to be expected and thus the final decision may change accordingly.

The problem of specifying *whose* interests are at stake, or *to whom* the investment is worthwhile, is more complex when public projects are considered. For example, *should* a state highway agency, in deciding among various highway projects (including the null alternative), consider only the consequences to the state highway users or those to the entire state populace, or should it adopt a broader national point of view? Also, *should* the state highway agency consider the economic feasibility of only the *state agency's* expenditures on construction, maintenance, and administration or should it be concerned with the feasibility of the total outlays and with the overall consequences, whether state, federal, or local and whether public or private?

The arguments for and against different viewpoints are numerous. E.L. Grant persuasively argues that the economy of public works proposals (whether city, county, or state) "ideally, perhaps," should be considered from the point of view of all of the people in the country.[7] T.E. Kuhn takes what at first glance appears to be a stronger stand.[8] While he makes no distinction between local, state, or federal (public) agencies, and thus implies that *all* public agencies (whether local, county, state, or federal) *should* take the *national* economy viewpoint, the manner in which he distinguishes between and treats internal and external costs and gains (benefits) elsewhere in his text, does suggest that at times he feels it is proper for a public agency to view only the costs and benefits to its own economy. This implication is supported by his metropolitan transport example wherein intergovernment transfers are treated as benefits.[9]

An alternative position might be to consider the feasibility from the point of view of *those whose funds or resources are being risked.* That is, the feasibility might be judged in terms of the welfare of those who must bear the burden of having foregone more worthwhile opportunities, or of financing capital investments or future operating expenses, should the expected benefits not materialize. This would appear to be the position of Richard Zettel, who noted:[10]

The appropriate objective is to maximize benefits to the users who are called upon to finance the programme. ... In some circumstances ... it may be appropriate to seek contributions from the general treasury to finance that portion of the project which is justified on the grounds of general (rather than user) benefit.

Thus, with a pay-as-you-go or fully self-financed highway user tax-financing program, only the user's viewpoint would appear to be relevant. However, should the highway program be financed out of general state or federal funds (or should highway bonds be floated and backed by the full faith and credit of the state or federal government), then the viewpoint of the entire state or federal populace would be appropriate. To take the point of view of those whose funds or resources are being risked will result in taking a "total public viewpoint," but the definition does permit a more restrictive position to be taken where it is appropriate (such as with privately financed toll facilities or with public facilities supported entirely through user tax revenues).[11]

Another important and associated aspect is the establishment of the yard-sticks, or measures, by which the worthwhileness or feasibility of a project can be judged. It would be my view that worthwhileness should be defined from the point of view of the "owners" or those whose funds or resources are being risked. Thus, an answer to the question, "Worthwhile in What Terms?," would have three parts:

(1) What specific factors or elements which are affected by the project do the "owners" (i.e., those whose resources are being risked) feel are of importance and of concern; these are the items of "cost" or "benefit";

(2) What is the relative importance or relative value which the "owners" attach to the particular items of "cost" or "benefit" (i.e., what are the weights to be used in placing the "cost" and "benefit" items on a commensurate value scale); and

(3) What are the constraints (if any, and which are over and above any constraints which may be imposed by a higher authority) which the "owners" place on the system and which will or may affect the decision-making outcome.[f]

It should be evident that such a task for private projects is distinctly simpler and more straightforward than for public programs. Generally, "costs" for private projects include money outlays which must be made to obtain the capital, labor, and service inputs, or to compensate others for damages of one sort or another; the "benefits" include the money revenues (or other types of payment) received as a result of the project investment.[g] Thus, only items which in some way are actually translated into money terms are usually included in the economic analysis.

For the case of public projects at the Federal level, all factors or elements of concern which have value to the "owning" public and for which value the public would willingly pay (in a broad sense) to gain, or to keep from losing, will be included. Thus, commonly-thought-of social and political objectives can meaningfully be included in an economy study, provided of course that the owning public would be willing to pay for such or at least to trade-off some other object of interest or value where conflicts occur.[h] Generally, then, social or political factors should enter the analysis only in those instances where society would be

---

[f]Rather than include some arbitrary objective alongside the other terms and give it some relative scale value, the "owners" may prefer merely to maximize their net benefit, for example, subject to some specified condition. In a sense, this specification would be somewhat analogous to certain types of government regulation, and is directly akin to establishing certain social objectives *regardless of the impacts.* While these constraints, or social objectives, will not directly enter the economic analysis, their economic consequences should be accounted for in the overall decision-making process; the economic value of social objectives can at least be determined by imputation, for example.

[g]In some cases, this narrow description will not be all inclusive.

[h]This position will be qualified in a later section in order to preserve comparability between private and public investment policy.

willing to forego dollar-and-cent or other values in their stead. This assumption is made, first, since most tangible and so-called intangible objects of concern have a history of experience and have been valued at the marketplace (at least implicitly); thus, there is a place to start in establishing relative if not absolute value scales (a problem that simply cannot be ignored, one way or another). Second, this assumption is made to point out that factors of *presumed* concern to the owning public, and for which they are *not* willing to forego something else of value (which *must* be foregone to achieve the object of concern), are just that—presumed rather than real. Third, it is made in order to permit more reasonable comparisons among investments in the private and public sectors of the economy.

By this discussion, it is not implied that decisions involving other "political" or "social" values are improper or avoidable. Rather, it is to emphasize that decisions to expend additional resources in order to meet or achieve some higher social goal or objective imply at least a limiting value of the social ends (since the extra costs could have been avoided by sacrificing the social objective). Also, the earlier remarks were intended to emphasize that lack of willingness to "pay" for some social objective (or at least to forego something else of value in order to achieve that goal) suggests the lack of real value associated with the objective. In any case, the planner or analyst bears the responsibility of defining and quantifying (directly or by imputation) as many of these aspects as possible.

Also, with such a broad view being taken of the highway transport problem and of public investment in highway facilities, one might ask whether it is appropriate to include within the analysis and framework some consideration of other city planning (or community) objectives, and to account for any interactions between highway transport investment and the spatial organization of business, industry, and residence and resultant economic or social effects. Clearly, these system effects should be part of the overall system analysis if the public welfare (in terms of economic efficiency or incidence of costs and benefits) is affected over and above that as measured by examining overall transportation costs and benefits. While these sorts of external effects differ only in character and extent from other more readily identifiable externalities which stem from transportation facility improvement and usage (such as air pollution), it must be said that it is considerably more difficult to establish (at least with any reliability) cause and effect transportation and land-use relationships; in fact, the present state of the art in transportation and land-use planning is such that, at best, only limited statistical correlations can be shown and only approximate and tentative hypotheses about causal relationships can be made. Accordingly, little attempt will be made to introduce these diverse sorts of planning issues (unless there appears to be sufficiently strong evidence of dependent relationships and of measurable and identifiable externalities).

1.4 Preview of Investment Planning Analysis

The investment problem described earlier will be discussed and analyzed, first in terms of its components, and second in terms of the relationships among components. Also, the investment problem will be viewed in successive stages of complexity, beginning with the analysis that is applicable to situations in which the demand and travel conditions are regarded as static or constant over time, and extending to the analysis which is appropriate under more dynamic and changing conditions of demand and tripmaking. Finally, attention will be centered on the problems and consequences which stem from implementing various types of pricing and control mechanisms, and on the way in which investment planning may be affected by these problems.

More explicitly, in Chapter 2 the items of transport cost which bear on public investment planning will be detailed; further, the functional relationships for costs will be described in sufficient detail to differentiate between those cost items which vary with changes in output or tripmaking levels only on some long-run basis (that is, over fairly long periods of time), and those which vary with changes in output on an hour to hour or day to day basis. Also, attention will be focused upon the differences between those transport costs which are privately perceived by tripmakers and those which result from their tripmaking but are not privately perceived; these distinctions will be necessary to later discussions of travel forecasting and of determining price levels for economic efficiency. Finally, the subject of selecting a proper discount or interest rate will be surveyed.

In Chapter 3, the functional relationships between tripmaking (or quantity of travel demanded) and trip price will be described, both for situations of static or constant demand and for those in which demand varies from hour to hour and year to year. (Price should be construed as the total trip payment in time, effort, and money.) Also, the use of these demand functions for determining travel benefits and revenues will be described. Once these demand and benefit conditions have been detailed, the subject of travel forecasting or of determining the actual tripmaking volume and travel price, for particular facilities and for specific pricing conditions, will be undertaken. These interrelationships will be described for both static and dynamic demand conditions, and thus will permit accounting of peak- and off-peak-loading conditions and of year to year shifts or increases in tripmaking. The final section of Chapter 3 will include an example problem dealing with the joint determination of toll rates and actual tripmaking volumes in situations where demand fluctuates from hour to hour; this problem will illustrate the detailed information requisite to such an analysis, as well as the precise way in which cost, demand, and price conditions are interrelated.

In Chapter 4, the discussion will center on matters involving economic efficiency and will relate investment planning and pricing policy to facility utilization and to economic and financial feasibility. Initially, these problems will be handled on a segmented basis in which pricing and facility planning (or benefit-cost analysis) procedures will be individually formulated for situations with: (1) constant demand; (2) year to year (or intertemporal) demand fluctuations; and (3) hour to hour (or intratemporal) demand fluctuations. Immediately following, the overall investment and pricing problem will be formulated for situations involving both hour to hour and year to year demand fluctuations. Also, this chapter will include a brief treatment of the complications which are added and which are caused by capacity-reducing types of facilities (that is, by facilities in which shock-wave action can cause the capacity to be reduced).

In the concluding chapter, some of the practical difficulties which stem from implementing the procedures and models formulated previously will be examined, and modifications will be included to permit the analyst to account for these effects. Finally, a brief discussion will touch upon and highlight other important issues which relate to investment planning and which can affect the analysis and decision-making process in important ways.

2

Transport Cost Functions

To accomplish the objective of providing "useful and worthwhile" devices or facilities, engineers in conjunction with economists (and others) must: (1) describe the various technological means of constructing, operating, and maintaining the device or facility; (2) determine the human and material resources required for its construction and operation and for passenger movement thereon; and (3) determine the cost of the resource inputs. Clearly, such a task is not accomplished in the abstract, or aside from consideration of the facility performance characteristics (either in terms of output or service) and of the facility's overall desirability to the buying public. The particular alternatives which are examined and costed in detail are chosen because their performance and cost characteristics are expected to be compatible with market conditions. In spite of this fact, the discussion in this chapter will deal with production and cost functions in a more abstract fashion.

It will be necessary to introduce a number of issues which normally are ignored by engineers but nonetheless are of vital importance to the proper determination of the transport costs (within the context of public welfare). Such aspects include those of opportunity costs, external costs and benefits, social rate of discount, taxes, and risk aversion. These aspects, while important, will only be touched upon, rather than being covered thoroughly.

2.1 General Description of Production and Cost Functions[1]

Production functions describe the relationship between facility or system output and the required resource inputs (i.e., man hours of labor; tons of gravel, steel, and cement; etc.) and they serve as the first step to determine cost functions. Once the unit prices of acquiring the resource inputs are determined and applied to the production functions inputs, the cost function or relationship between cost and output can be established.

The engineer and economist must determine for each possible level of output and service the most efficient or least costly technological solution (in broad terms and without regard for the incidence of the costs). The production and cost functions have a direct relationship to the time dimension or to the time available for adjusting the technology. For example, over the short-run or over a short period of time (such as a day or week), the only opportunity available is to make the best use of the existing facilities or existing plant capacity or to make

11

limited marginal improvements to the existing facility. Either the production or cost functions for the short-run situation may be far different from those for the long-run (i.e., over a long period of time such as a year or more), during which time it will be possible to expand the facility or plant capacity or to take advantage of new technologies.[2]

Another way of thinking about the distinction between short-run and long-run cost functions would be as follows: a short-run cost function describes the relationship between cost and output for a particular facility at a given point in time and thus can be used for determining the actual operating conditions and costs; the long-run cost function by representing the relationship among costs, output, *and* facility size or capacity aids significantly in the investment planning process. Thus, one may think of the short-run cost curve as a guide for operating decisions and the long-run cost curve as a guide for planning decisions.

The problem of determining the most efficient or least costly technology *for a given level of output* (and time period) is of course analogous to the usual engineering design problem in which the least annual cost design solution is sought by comparing various payment types or thicknesses, etc., and by making tradeoffs between technologies, between materials and labor, or between facility and vehicle operating or user travel costs until the least costly design is determined. While most engineers make these kinds of calculations within the context of benefit-cost analysis, herein it will be assumed that the *production* and cost functions represent the minimum cost possibilities for the specified levels of output and thus that no other (profitable) engineering design changes can be made for the specified output and time period conditions.

The difficulties and complexities of converting the required input of material and labor resources into costs will not be a subject for discussion here except to mention two aspects: (1) it will be necessary to account for absolute or relative changes in the cost of labor or material inputs that occur over time; and (2) it will be necessary to distinguish between market prices and opportunity costs where they differ. Regarding the latter, on occasion market prices may overstate or understate the value which the forfeited resources have or would have in alternative opportunities or uses; in these instances market prices should be replaced by "shadow prices" or prices which are more appropriate measures of the real opportunity cost to society of the inputs.[3]

Once production functions have been formulated by the engineer, and prices (or opportunity costs) determined for the inputs, cost functions can generally be stated as follows:

$$\text{Cost} = f(\text{output, capacity level}) \quad . \tag{2-1}$$

However, to properly characterize the costs such that they may be related to investment, demand, and pricing considerations, several important aspects must be accounted for. First, the entire stream of expenditures which stem from the construction and operation of a facility must be analyzed, both in terms of the long-run commitment of resources, and in terms of the year in which the various expenditures are made. Also, it should be emphasized that the initial capital outlays are different from future annual operating expenses only in terms of the time at which the expenditures are required. In other words, an investment policy is concerned with the long-term commitments and not solely with the initial capital outlays; in this sense, present expenditures are no more important than future ones (aside, of course, from the uncertainties of the future and the obvious time difference and alternative uses of resources in the interim). Second, an analysis period or planning horizon must be defined or settled upon; in general, the selection of an analysis period will be arbitrary but will be related to the uncertainties of the activity being analyzed and to the replacement requirements. In regard to the latter point, if the analysis period is so long relative to the service lives of the various capital components that replacement of certain capital components is required, it will be necessary to represent the replacement costs in terms of the technology and input or factor prices which are expected at the time of replacement. (The engineer, to date, has tended to regard the future replacement costs as being equal to the present costs, and to ignore technological improvements and changes in the relative and absolute prices of future labor and material inputs.) Third, it will be particularly important, though difficult, to establish a proper relationship between the long-term expenditures (which are made for the output over n years) and the facility output measure and demand functions, the latter of which generally will be formulated on an hourly *unit time* basis for the yth year and will vary for $y = 1, \ldots, n$.

To point out how difficulties arise with respect to the unit time basis for demand functions, consider the relationship between long-term expenditures, changes in facility output, and the duration and year of such changes. To be able to represent the interaction between facility output, facility capacity, and congestion (and thus part of travel cost), it is necessary to measure flow or output over a fairly small unit time interval or, say, an hour. As the facility output increases (for a facility of fixed capacity), there generally will be some increase in the long-term expenditures, but the extent of the increase will depend on the year in which the output increases[a] and on the duration of the increase (i.e., the number of hours in which the flow is increased). More will be said about this point later in the discussion.

Putting aside some of the above difficulties for the time being, let us characterize the (short-run) cost function for a facility of capacity x as follows:

$$TC_x(q) = F_x + VC_x(q) \quad, \tag{2-2}$$

---

[a] In other words, expenditures in the future will be less costly than those in the present, everything else being equal.

where

TC_x (q) = total costs for q trips per hour on facility x

F_x = fixed costs (or opportunity costs)[b] for facility x

VC_x (q) = variable costs for q trips per hour on facility x.

(Also, for the moment, assume that the fixed costs F_x are scaled in terms of the *hourly* fixed cost.) The distinction between fixed and variable costs is, simply, that for a particular facility the former (or F_x) are fixed with respect to output and do not vary with changes in usage which the xth facility may or does experience, while the latter (or variable costs) vary or change with usage or increases in output. (Alternatively, the "fixed" costs may be viewed as those costs which are nonseparable with respect to nonzero output levels and thus are common to all units of output.) In turn, unit costs can be computed as follows:

$$atc_x \ (q) = TC_x \ (q)/q = \left[F_x + VC_x(q) \right]/q \qquad (2\text{-}3)$$

$$avc_x \ (q) = VC_x \ (q)/q \qquad (2\text{-}4)$$

$$mc_x \ (q) \ \dot{=} \ \frac{dTC_x \ (q)}{dq}$$

$$\dot{=} \ \frac{dVC_x \ (q)}{dq} \ , \qquad (2\text{-}5)^c$$

atc_x (q) = *average total* cost per trip for q trips per hour on facility x

avc_x (q) = *average variable* cost per trip for q trips per hour on facility x

mc_x (q) = *marginal cost* (at flow q), or increase in total costs on facility x when flow is increased from q to $q + 1$ trips per hour.

These cost relationships may be seen in Figure 2-1.[d] Note that the marginal cost is dependent only upon the variable costs (for this fixed-capacity facility) and that the marginal cost is equal to the average total cost when the average total cost function is at its minimum cost point. Below that point, the marginal cost is lower than the average total cost, and above it, the reverse holds true. Also, the

---

[b]That is, the opportunity costs of those items which are nonseparable or fixed with respect to the output level or to changes in that level for $q > 0$.

[c]Use of a differential represents an approximation for $\frac{\Delta TC_x(q)}{\Delta q}$, since q can assume only integer values.

[d]Throughout, only "well behaved" cost functions will be dealt with, other than for the backward bending capacity case, which will be discussed later; this assumption does little (if any) harm to the conceptual and practical details of the development.

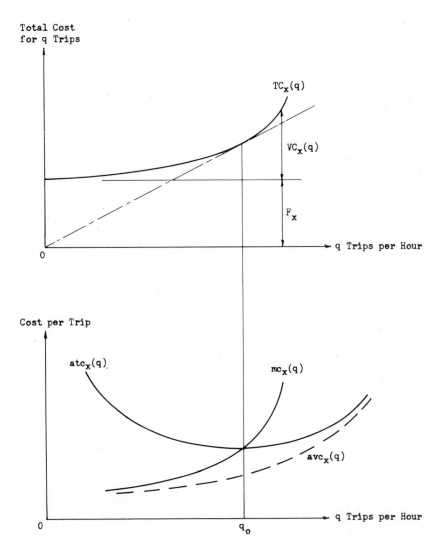

Figure 2-1. Basic Cost Functions and Relationships.

average variable cost is always lower than the average total cost, but at high flow levels they are practically equal to each other.

It should be reemphasized that marginal cost is the increase in total costs (for all $q + 1$ vehicles, as a group) incurred as the flow level q is increased by one trip per hour; thus, the marginal cost has no relationship to fixed cost. Referring to Figure 2-2, it can be shown that for any flow q_1 :[e]

$$\sum_{q=1}^{q_1} mc_x(q) = \left[q_1\right] \cdot \left[avc_x(q_1)\right] = VC_x(q_1) \ , \tag{2-6}$$

and, therefore, that the two shaded areas in Figure 2-2 are equal. (This areal relationship will be helpful at a later stage when pricing is discussed.)

The specification of output units is of some considerable importance to these cost functions (as well as the demand functions) and needs clarification. Throughout this book, output will be thought of as "vehicle trips per hour." Two important qualifications must be stressed, however. One, this output (or, say, q trips per hour) will consist of q *separate and different* vehicles making use of the facility during an hour.[f] Two, it will be assumed that each of the q vehicle

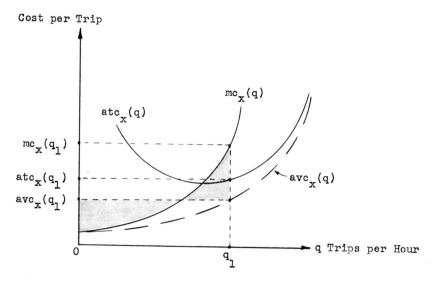

Figure 2-2. (Short-Run) Cost Relationships for Facility X.

---

[e]The marginal costs are summed over all nonzero levels of output and thus do not include any fixed or nonseparable costs which do not vary with (nonzero) output changes.

[f]In essence, travelers will be making dichotomous decisions about whether or not to make a trip on a particular facility within a specific hour, rather than making decisions about how many trips to make during an hour.

trips using a particular facility during any hour will be identical with respect to the number of passengers or travelers riding in each vehicle.[g] Finally, within this text all of the terms "trips," "tripmakers," "tripmaking" or "travelers" will be considered as being equivalent to vehicle trips as described above, unless specific mention is made to the contrary.

For this discussion, one may regard these "fixed capacity" cost relationships as *short-run* cost functions, since it is assumed that the time period is too short to alter the fixed capacity and thus to lower the total cost function. That is to say that in the short-run only the congestion (and other variable) costs will vary with changes in usage or flow levels. *Over the long-run*, however, the facility capacity and cost relationships can be altered (both upward and downward), thus changing the short-run cost functions as well. Let us consider the long-run cost relationships (or planning cost functions) in two steps, first while analyzing the cost functions for facilities of just three facility capacity levels and second while considering the entire range of capacity possibilities. The first of these conditions is shown in Figure 2-3 in which facility (0) is assumed to represent the cost conditions for an existing facility.

Several comments are in order regarding these three facility (plant) sizes. First, it should be noted that the fixed cost (F_0) for the *existing* facility does not represent the initial capital outlays for that facility, but is the opportunity cost for the facility, land, or other marketable features; simply, F_0 represents the value of the existing facility and land in its best alternative use and thus the foregone opportunity if it is retained in transport service. Second, it should be evident that for these three possible cases it would be less costly to expand the existing facility to the level of facility (1), if the flow q were expected to be between q_e and q_f, and if the existing facility were not to be abandoned (regardless of its feasibility).[h] Similarly, among the three capacity cases, expanded facility (2) is the less costly for expected flows above q_f.

The heavy line in Figure 2-3(a) defines the *long-run total cost function* which is applicable for facility expansion and planning purposes. That is, over the long-run we can expand capacity such that the total costs for flow q are defined by the heavy line. Of more significance, the slope of the long-run *total* cost function is, by definition, the *long-run marginal cost* curve and is the *heavy* "saw-toothed" solid line in part (b) of Figure 2-3.

As illustrated in Figure 2-3(b), the dashed portion of the marginal cost curves together with the heavy solid line portion defines the *short-run* marginal cost for

---

[g]This assumption, while certainly unrealistic, is necessary for the development which follows in this and the next chapter; also, it is (implicitly) embodied within the assumption of homogeneous travel and congestion costs as detailed in Chapter 1. While the assumption can be relaxed, to do so would require an analytical structure extending far beyond that pursued here.

[h]In short, here we are merely examining which alternative is less costly at specified levels of output; none are examined in terms of overall feasibility. Also, for the moment, both the scaling problem mentioned earlier and variable demand situations are overlooked.

18

(a) Total Cost Functions

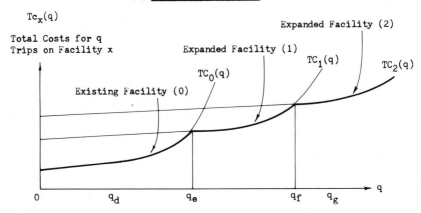

$Tc_x(q)$

Total Costs for q
Trips on Facility x

Existing Facility (0)

$TC_0(q)$

Expanded Facility (1)

Expanded Facility (2)

$TC_1(q)$

$TC_2(q)$

q_d q_e q_f q_g

q

0

(b) Marginal and Average Total Cost Functions

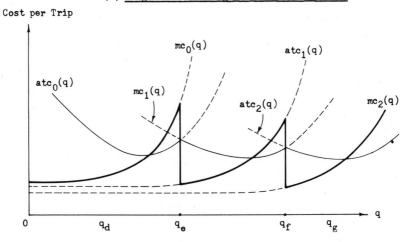

Cost per Trip

$atc_0(q)$

$mc_0(q)$

$atc_1(q)$

$mc_1(q)$

$atc_2(q)$

$mc_2(q)$

0   q_d q_e q_f q_g q

Figure 2–3. Cost Functions for Three Facility Sizes.

the particular facility to which it refers. For example, suppose that the existing facility were expanded to the level of facility (1) because of long-run demand expectations as related to long-run total cost conditions. Once the facility has been expanded, only the short-run marginal cost curve or $mc_1(q)$ is relevant for determining the cost increases associated with increases in flow q for that facility.

Again, to clarify the relationship between average total cost and marginal cost, both for short-run and long-run situations, the two sets of average total-cost curves are also shown in Figure 2-3(b); the *long-run* average total-cost curve is the *light* solid line, whereas the dashed and solid line portions together represent the short-run average total-cost curve for a particular facility.

For the situation shown in Figure 2-3 in which there is an existing facility, the incremental costs of expanding facility capacity and output beyond some nonzero output level can be determined simply by summing the long-run marginal costs between the before and after output levels. As an example, let us find the *incremental* costs (i.e., the additional fixed and variable costs) which result from expanding the output level from q_d to q_g (where $0 < q_d < q_e$ and $q_g > q_f$).[i] For this case, the incremental costs or IC_{dg} will be as follows:

$$IC_{dg} = TC_2(q_g) - TC_0(q_d) , \qquad (2\text{-}7)$$

in which $TC_2(q_g)$ is:

$$TC_2(q_g) = TC_2(q_f) + \sum_{q=q_f}^{q_g} mc_2(q) , \qquad (2\text{-}8)$$

and similarly by substituting for $TC_2(q_f)$ in equation (2-8),

$$TC_2(q_g) = TC_0(q_e) + \sum_{q=q_e}^{q_f} mc_1(q) + \sum_{q=q_f}^{q_g} mc_2(q) . \qquad (2\text{-}9)$$

Relating $TC_0(q_e)$ and $TC_0(q_d)$, it can be seen that:

$$TC_0(q_e) = TC_0(q_d) + \sum_{q=q_d}^{q_e} mc_0(q) \qquad (2\text{-}10a)$$

and, therefore,

$$TC_0(q_d) = TC_0(q_e) - \sum_{q=q_d}^{q_e} mc_0(q) . \qquad (2\text{-}10b)$$

---

[i] *Incremental* costs, as used herein, may be defined as the increase in total costs which occurs as output is increased by *more than one* output unit, whereas marginal cost refers to the increase in total cost which occurs when output is increased by *just one* output unit.

Substituting equations (2-9) and (2-10b) into equation (2-7), the incremental costs incurred when the output is increased from q_d to q_g are:

$$IC_{dg} = \sum_{q=q_d}^{q_e} mc_0\,(q) + \sum_{q=q_e}^{q_f} mc_1\,(q) + \sum_{q=q_s}^{q_g} mc_2\,(q) \ . \ \text{(2-11)}$$

Thus, the incremental costs of adjusting facility capacity and expanding the output level beyond some nonzero output level (over the long-run) can be determined solely (and if desired) by examining variable cost data. This is not to say that consideration of the fixed costs associated with different levels of output is unimportant; rather, the fixed costs are directly related to a determination of the most efficient technology and of the appropriate cost function for the various levels of output, and therefore of the long-run marginal cost curve. Furthermore, the fixed costs are significantly involved in matters of both economic and financial feasibility, in matters of pricing policy, and in matters of facility abandonment. All of these problems will receive detailed treatment in later sections or chapters.

The cost functions characterized thus far, and in Figure 2-3, were those for highly *indivisible* technologies and implied that the expansion possibilities were greatly restricted and "lumpy;" or, in simpler terms, it was implied that capacity and service (which are joint products) can be expanded only in large increments or jumps. More realistically, though, if one considers the entire range of design features which *can* be altered by the engineer (e.g., number of lanes, width of lanes, lateral and vertical clearances, sight distance, gradient, radius of curvature, superelevation, surfacing, median widths, etc.) and which affect either capacity or travel service (speeds, accidents, etc.), in addition to the variability with respect to number of vehicles (and passengers) using the highway facility, it seems more reasonable to regard transport technologies—particularly for highway transport—as being highly divisible and as being capable of expansion in small if not virtually continuous increments.[j] By the same token, one can reason that capacity and service can be contracted or reduced in somewhat divisible increments, though probably not to the same degree as expansion. (Since contraction seems to be of less general importance than expansion, no major attempt will be made to justify the assumption of perfect or constant divisibility for contraction, an assumption which will be made hereafter.)

For perfectly divisible technological situations, the inclusion of the cost

---

[j]However, it should be noted that in present practice the engineer commonly sets or uses invariant engineering standards for many of the variables concerning the highway facility (e.g., lane widths, vertical clearances, etc.), thus causing some unevenness for the highway facility portion of the entire highway transport technology. Since the highway facility accounts for only a small portion (say, 10 to 20 percent) of the total cost function, though, it can be reasoned that even this self-imposed facility indivisibility will have little effect on the overall divisibility.

functions for all cases would result in the long-run marginal cost (and long-run average total cost) curve being changed from the saw-tooth (and scalloped) character shown in Figure 2-3 to the smooth curve of Figure 2-4. The short-run marginal cost and short-run average total-cost curves would remain exactly as before (except of course there are more of them); these short-run curves are also shown in Figure 2-4 for facility x. Hereafter, the long-run or planning curves will be designated by the prefix lr and short-run or operating ones by the prefix sr (lowercase will be used for the unit cost curves and capitals for the total cost curves).

The cost relationships illustrated in Figure 2-4 are not general cost functions, but are representative *only* for situations of perfect divisibility and of *constant returns to scale* (or constant economies of scale). The term "constant returns to scale" means that cost and output increase (or decrease) proportionately (i.e., a 10 percent increase in output will be accompanied by a 10 percent increase in total cost); thus it means that the average total cost will remain constant. For this special case, long-run marginal and long-run average total costs are equal and constant for all levels of output. Also, it should be pointed out that the long-run marginal cost corresponds to the cost occuring when the plant or facility is operated at its minimum-cost level of flow.

A more general (and probably more appropriate) long-run cost situation is illustrated in Figure 2-5, in which increasing returns to scale (or economies of scale) are exhibited for output levels below q_o and decreasing returns to scale (or diseconomies of scale) are exhibited for output above q_o.[k] In this instance, and in contrast to the constant returns case, the long-run marginal costs are equal to long-run average costs only for output level (or q_o) at which long-run average total costs are at a minimum. Further, for a plant size and facility output level other than for q_o, it should be stressed that the most efficient output level is not that which corresponds to the minimum short-run average total cost but that at which the short-run and long-run marginal cost are equal.[l] Referring to Figure 2-5, let us assume that demand (and other) conditions are such that over the long-run the facility's capacity should be adjusted to represent the most efficient (or least cost) alternative for an output level of q_a; thus, from the long-run total cost functions in Figure 2-5(a), facility x would be selected as the most efficient long-run possibility (i.e., any other alternative means higher cost for an output of q_a). Note, however, from Figure 2-5(b), that this "most efficient" output level (q_a) is below the output level (q_b) which corresponds to the minimum average total cost for this particular facility size, and thus results in a short-run

---

[k]Increasing returns to scale or economies of scale describe situations in which, proportionately, the total costs increase less than output, with increases in the latter; thus, the average total costs are decreasing. Decreasing returns to scale or diseconomies of scale are just the opposite; thus, with increases in output, the average total costs will increase.

[l]For the time being, assume that demand is constant and nonfluctuating, both intratemporally (or from hour to hour and day to day during some given year) and intertemporally (or from year to year).

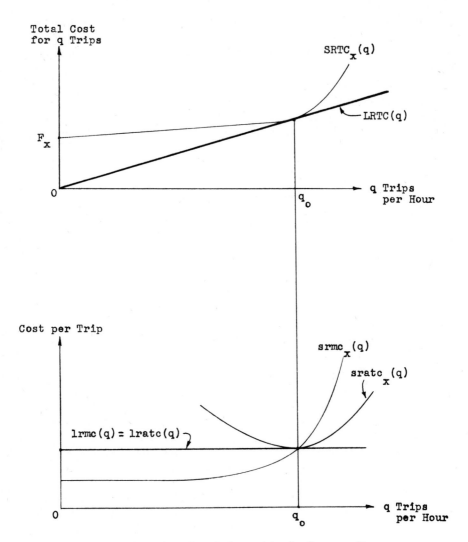

Figure 2-4. Long-Run Cost Relationships for Constant Returns.

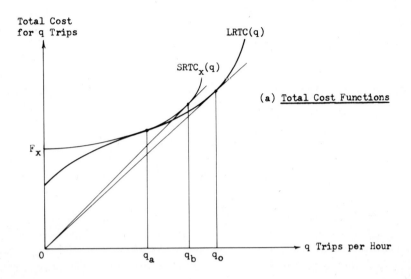

(a) <u>Total Cost Functions</u>

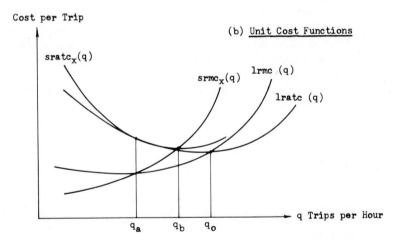

(b) <u>Unit Cost Functions</u>

Figure 2-5. Long-Run Cost Functions for Nonconstant Returns.

average total cost which is higher than one which could be achieved if this particular plant or facility were operated at output level q_b. The obvious question arises: Should facility x be operated at output level q_b instead of q_a if the plant is to be used most efficiently? Definitely not, at least for the conditions assumed thus far. That is, if the long-run demand were such that an output level of q_b is "needed", or most feasible, to put it more properly, then the total cost for that level of output could be reduced more by expanding the facility capacity than by operating facility x at its short-run minimum average total-cost output level. This can be seen simply by comparing $sratc_x(q_b)$ with $lratc(q_b)$ and noting that the latter is smaller, thereby indicating that total cost savings would accrue to the q_b tripmakers if the facility were expanded further instead of operating facility x at a higher output level.

2.2 Detailed Description and Makeup of Transport Cost Functions

In characterizing transport cost functions, at least for tripmaking over public ways, costs will be construed quite broadly and will include all private and public resources expended or forfeited for a specified amount of tripmaking. Thus, cost functions will include not only the labor and material inputs required to provide and maintain the vehicles and facilities or ways, but also will include the travel time, effort, and hazard costs which are expended by the travelers for their tripmaking.[4] Essentially, public agencies are involved in the process of trading-off public facility and private travel costs and of balancing incremental (public and private) transport costs and trip benefits. While such a construct clearly has more applicability in the public than in the private sector of the economy, the overall analysis is greatly simplified by its employment.

Specifically, by the inclusion of private travel time, effort, and hazard within the cost function, rather than by adding service dimensions to the demand functions, the structural relationships and ultimate ability to grasp the interactions are greatly simplified and enhanced.[5]

The cost functions to be described in this section will generally include the following items:

1. Fixed (or nonseparable) facility and social dislocation costs
2. Variable facility costs
3. Fixed vehicle ownership costs (to include terminal costs)
4. Variable vehicle costs
5. Variable travel time, effort, and hazard costs
6. Other costs (e.g., external diseconomies).

The last cost item, "other costs," warrants some additional explanation. Generally, it is meant to include so-called *external costs or diseconomies*, or costs which are imposed on others as a result of the transport facility or movement upon it and costs to which the others are not a party;[6] examples of such losses for transport situations would be air pollution and noise costs for nontravelers. Clearly, these types of externalities are not unique to public situations, but apply equally to both public and private sectors. (Consider, for example, the effects of noise, air, or stream pollution caused by either your neighbor or a private firm.) The problem in the first instance is to identify the magnitude of the cost[7] (for which there currently is no satisfactory market-place), and secondly, is to develop the institutional devices which will ascertain (whether and) how these costs are to be taken into account. Of equal importance, analysts, more often than not, simply include *either* the external costs *or* the external benefits, depending on which side of the issue they stand. Also, it should be recognized that to properly account for the externalities in the public sector, but not in the private sector, is to establish a double standard for investment policy and, thus, to at least permit inefficient decisions and improper allocation of investments to be made (as between the public and private sectors).

First, it is evident that externalities *should be*, but usually are not, accounted for in both the public and private sectors, thus introducing the practical problem of analyzing both the relative *and* overall worth (to the public) of public investment projects. For determining the overall worth or economic feasibility of public investments, all externalities should be properly measured and accounted for in computing the (discounted) total net benefit; clearly, those public projects with negative total net benefit, after inclusion of external costs and benefits (but with a positive total before their inclusion), should be rejected—even if externalities are not treated for private investment.[m] On the other hand, if externalities are included only for public projects, no clearcut statement can be made regarding the relative worth or desirability of investment as between the public and private sectors. Thus, inconsistent treatment can distort resource allocation as between the two sectors. However, such a position must be modified if there is sufficient reason to believe that externalities would only (or primarily) arise with respect to public investment situations;[n] in this instance, of course, the overall worth of public projects and that relative to allocation between public and private sectors would be properly accounted for simply by including all external costs and benefits stemming from public projects.

Second, there can be no doubt but that the measurement of external costs is extremely difficult and somewhat judgmental, if at all possible, particularly in the absence of market mechanisms to provide even approximate indications of real losses. However, as a means of estimating the external costs, one might argue that a reasonable proxy would be to determine the resource costs required to eliminate the nuisance or to reduce it to a "tolerable" level. In the first instance, the likelihood of overstating the external cost is high, while in the second, it can

---

[m]Assuming that there are no significant feedback effects.
[n]Increasingly, there seems to be little reason to believe that such an assumption is valid.

easily be overstated or understated—depending on one's judgment of "tolerable." (More will be said about this in Chapter 5.) And, finally, in matters of this sort, it is far too easy (if not common) to improperly label income transfers as external costs and thus to double-count[8] (i.e., one man or group loses, but another gains to an equal extent, thus resulting in no real loss or external cost to society).

All in all, while the analyst should make every attempt to measure and include all external costs *and* benefits in the evaluation of public projects, he should remain apprised of the possible inconsistencies and inaccuracies which can result from failure to examine the circumstances for both public and private sectors and from estimating the external effects.

Additional discussion is warranted with respect to some of the other transport cost items. First, these cost items generally apply to the short-run cost functions or the cost functions for a particular facility (or plant size). Second, though more will be said about this point, the costs should be thought of as those pertaining to a particular pattern of flow or output and occurring during some particular year (or at some more specific point in time).

The fixed facility costs for a new or expanded facility will include the costs for construction, land acquisition, and social dislocation (that is, the costs for moving displaced parties or firms or those for compensating disrupted people or firms); in those instances where the market prices do not reflect the true costs or the marginal opportunity costs, the market prices should be changed accordingly.[9] Particular care must be taken in evaluating either the cost of land which is being acquired for new or expanded facilities, or that of land being used for existing facilities and which continues to be used for transport facilities. Again, it is the marginal opportunity cost (or marginal cost in a perfectly competitive market situation where all of its alternative uses are properly considered) which is appropriate, rather than the market price or rather than a zero price, if the land is already being used for an existing transport facility or if it is public property.[o] Also, for those structural facility items which wear out only with time rather than use, and which must be replaced in some later year (but during the analysis period), the analyst must be careful to use the factor prices[p] and

---

[o]It seems likely that the land acquisition costs employed in engineering cost studies are usually below the proper opportunity cost. In a similar vein, it is also likely that the vehicle ownership costs are overstated (that is, higher than the marginal opportunity costs). More specifically, in the former case one often finds that engineers evaluate the cost of land used for transport facilities (especially that for existing facilities or that which is converted from other public uses) below the value which it would have had in alternative private, commercial, or other public uses (such as use for zoos, recreational areas, or schools). In the case of evaluating vehicle ownership costs, it would seem that use of market prices paid for automobile purchases, or cash flow payments for those autos purchased on installment plans, would lead to an overstatement of the opportunity costs. Such a conclusion rests upon the fairly certain assumption that lack of perfect competition in the automobile industry has resulted in auto purchase prices being above the marginal opportunity cost, and that less than perfect information and knowledge about discounting practices and effective interest rates for many installment loan plans has led buyers to pay more than opportunity costs for autos.

[p]Factor prices are the opportunity costs of the material or labor inputs (wherein the material or labor inputs are often referred to as the factors of production).

appropriate technologies for that later point in time, rather than simply assume that the replacement costs will be equal to the initial ones.

The fixed vehicle costs present a reasonably difficult problem because of the complexities in establishing the relationship between vehicle ownership and tripmaking on specific facilities. For example, as a new facility is built or an existing facility expanded, does increased automobile ownership result which otherwise would not have occurred? Or do people merely make more frequent trips? And how is ownership and usage related to the facility size? In certain of these situations, the vehicle ownership costs could be regarded as variable rather than fixed costs (that is, they would be regarded as variable and thus separable with respect to changes in output), while in others, it would be more appropriate to regard them as being fixed. For instance, that portion of vehicle ownership costs which does not depreciate with use (i.e., that portion which is not variable with tripmaking or mileage) could be regarded as fixed in those instances where output increases merely represented more frequent tripmaking by the same vehicle owners. By contrast, if increases in output are regarded as new tripmakers and if they require additional vehicles to be put into use, the vehicle ownership costs might be regarded as variable with respect to output. The latter type of situation would be more appropriate for work-trip commuting, for example, and in those instances where a constant and repetitive day-to-day or week-to-week pattern is followed by the same group of travelers. Also, the relative ease and quickness with which travelers can switch over to other modes, or from driver to car pooler, and can sell used cars, probably induces drivers to take a longer-term view of their private variable costs rather than simply to account for the very short-term day to day out-of-pocket travel expenditures (in time, money and effort).[q]

At any rate, for the purposes of this discussion, it will be assumed that the vehicle ownership costs (to include the associated terminal costs) can be placed on a variable "per vehicle trip" basis, along with the vehicle operating and maintenance costs.[r]

---

[q]While these are but very tentative hypotheses, some comfort might be taken from the fact that about 60 percent of new car buyers and 44 percent of used car buyers use installment loans to make their purchases, and thus receive monthly reminders of the auto purchase and use costs (which are probably higher than the opportunity costs). On the other hand, the picture is complicated by resale considerations, and related matters.

[r]If the market purchase and resale prices were good signals of real costs, the ownership cost per trip—for this situation—could be computed as follows:

$$\text{Cost per vehicle trip} = [(P - L)\ (crf_{i,m}) + (L)(i)]\ /N,$$

where $crf_{i,m}$ is the capital recovery factor as shown in equation (2-12), P is the initial purchase price of the auto, L is the resale value of the auto at the end of m years, i is the discount rate, and N is the number of vehicle trips made annually. However, this formulation implicitly assumes that the auto is replaced every m years, under virtually identical purchase and resale conditions. On the other hand, this disadvantage can be overcome by making use of the procedure outlined in the footnote accompanying equation (2-12).

For all of these cost items, *no* taxes or excises should be included, other than to the extent that they are representative of, and proxies for, other directly associated resource costs (such as those for policing or administration).

Without much doubt, the most difficult costs to measure reliably are the variable travel time, effort, and hazard costs which are associated with different levels of tripmaking (or output) and with facilities of varying capacity. There is no necessity for recounting the difficulties of properly assessing these cost components or for emphasizing the importance of doing so, other than to repeat the extent to which the entire analysis hinges on their measurement. For example, the average costs for urban auto passenger trips—other than for travel time and effort costs—have been estimated as ranging between 12 and 14 cents per passenger mile at overall door-to-door speeds of about 30 mph for *downtown* trips averaging about 6 miles in length; for this case, travel time costs of only 2 cents per minute, for example, would represent about 25 percent of the total costs and time costs of 4 cents per minute would be almost 40 percent of the total. For urban trips in general, in which the parking costs do not loom so large (they represent about one-half of the above costs, time being excluded), the time costs assume an even greater importance.[10] While the research on this score is far from complete or even reliable, it appears reasonable to expect these costs to range between 4 and 6 cents per vehicle-trip mile on the average[11] and thus to be of crucial importance.

Beyond noting or assuming an approximate form and a certain functional interrelationship for these cost items, no major attempt will be made herein to describe them accurately or specifically.[12] This formulation is probably an oversimplification, but will still be useful in portraying the cost relationships and indicating their interaction with demand functions, and almost certainly will do no harm to the rationale which stems from the formulation.

A final technical problem remains for discussion before any more detailed characterization of the cost functions is attempted. This problem regards the *time interval for the output measure* as it relates to cost and demand functions. Costs can be correctly computed only by relating the output or flow levels at *each point in time* to the particular characteristics of that facility, by accounting for changes in factor prices (or opportunity costs) over time, and by appropriately discounting future costs. In other words, given the output or flow pattern for each hour over time (assuming that this is the most appropriate unit time interval for output as related to the facility and its performance characteristics), the discounted costs for that pattern of flow and facility can be determined. Each different pattern of flow will (probably) have a different total discounted cost. As a consequence, cost functions of the sort to be used herein (and as illustrated in Figures 2-1 through 2-5) are appropriate or accurate only for the implied flow pattern.

To be more specific, it is necessary to use flow or tripmaking volume *per hour* as the output measure for transport situations, because of hourly fluctuations in demand, and because a larger unit time interval (such as volume *per day*) would not permit a realistic assessment of the actual travel and congestion conditions.[s] By use of this unit time interval for the output, it is implied that the hourly flow remains constant over the time period for which the total costs are aggregated. Though it is meaningful to examine the cost and demand interrelationships on a year-to-year basis, it would make little sense to aggregate the total costs on a year-to-year basis for this purpose;[t] that is, of concern is the total stream of expenditures over an analysis period (which may be 20 to 40 years) as related to the pattern of flow over that same period, rather than simply the total outlays in year 1 as related to the flow in year 1, the total outlays in year 2 as related to the flow in year 2, and so forth. Clearly, the difficulty arises mainly because of the fixed costs which, again, while being made at one point in time, are a long-term expenditure and committed because of the long-term flow expectations.

The simplest procedure for handling the fixed costs is to place them on an output time-interval basis by making use of capital recovery factors, which are defined as follows:[u]

$$crf_{i,n} = \frac{i(1+i)^n}{(1+i)^n - 1} = \frac{i}{(1+i)^n - 1} + i \quad , \tag{2-12}$$

in which $crf_{i,n}$ is the capital recovery factor for a n year analysis period and a discount rate of i (expressed as a decimal fraction). It should be recognized that the capital-recovery factor is equivalent to a sinking-fund factor plus interest; when the capital-recovery factor is multiplied by the fixed costs made in year 0 or by the fixed costs made over the n years but discounted to year 0, the product will be equal to the fixed costs per year.[v] These annual costs can be converted to an hourly (or any other time interval) basis by dividing by the number of hours in a year.

One final point on this matter. It seems desirable to use capital recovery

---

[s]For example, a volume of 50,000 vehicle trips per day on a four-lane highway will not ·permit determination of the congestion and travel time costs without first specifying the hourly pattern of flow; spread uniformly throughout the day, 50,000 vehicle trips per day would cause little or no congestion and the daily travel time costs would be small, but if four hours had flows of 6000 vehicle trips per hour, and the remaining 26,000 were spread uniformly, the total daily travel time costs undoubtedly would be much larger.

[t]However, once the *actual* flow pattern is known, hour by hour and year to year, then the discounted costs can be accumulated in a straightforward manner and no difficulties are involved. Here, though, our concern is in knowing the interaction between cost and demand, a very different matter.

[u]Use of this factor implies that the discount rate remains constant over the n year analysis period. Also, for fixed costs or outlays made other than at year 0, it will be necessary to first discount the fixed costs to the present (i.e., year 0), and then apply the factor; any salvage value can be handled in a similar fashion, though as a negative cost.

[v]The product (or, $crf_{i,n}$ times fixed costs) may be regarded as the equivalent annual cash flow payment; it is equivalent to the payment which is typically made on home mortgage or auto loans (although the $crf_{i,n}$ factor above assumes annual compounding and payment, and the usual home mortgage or auto loan assumes monthly compounding and payment).

rather than discounted costs for the year-to-year analysis *pertaining to cost and demand interaction*, since it will permit us to avoid the complications of discounting the year-to-year variable costs as well as discounting the year-to-year demand functions.[13]

Under all of the above circumstances, the short-run total cost function (that is, the cost function for a facility of fixed capacity or, say, facility x) may be formulated as follows:[14]

$$SRTC_x(q) = F_x + qb_xd + \frac{qfd}{v_x - a_xq} \quad, \qquad (2\text{-}13)$$

where $SRTC_x(q)$ is the total hourly cost for handling a flow of q (in vehicles per hour) on facility x; a_x is a travel-time performance parameter dependent upon the facility design and capacity; b_x is a cost parameter for those facility and vehicle costs which vary solely with the facility capacity and design and with q and d (the distance traveled in miles); and f is a cost parameter for the cost items which vary with the trip time;[W] v_x is the average travel speed under very light flow or volume conditions; as before, F_x is the hourly fixed cost for facility x of length d.

In turn, the short-run average total, average variable, and marginal costs for facility x, respectively, can be shown to be:

$$sratc_x(q) = F_x/q + b_xd + \frac{fd}{v_x - a_xq} \qquad (2\text{-}14)$$

$$sravc_x(q) = b_xd + \frac{fd}{v_x - a_xq} \qquad (2\text{-}15)$$

$$srmc_x(q) = b_xd + \frac{fd}{v_x - a_xq} + \frac{qfda_x}{(v_x - a_xq)^2} \qquad (2\text{-}16)$$

$$= b_xd + \frac{fdv_x}{(v_x - a_xq)^2} \qquad (2\text{-}17)$$

2.3 Selection of An Appropriate Discount Rate

Prescribing an "appropriate" discount or interest rate, while difficult, is of crucial importance to matters of economic efficiency, investment planning, and decision-making. Resources can be consumed now by the current generation or

---

[W]In this form, f is shown as constant and not dependent either on the trip length or on the level of congestion; clearly, this appears to be a gross oversimplification and should be altered.

conserved for future use by either the current or future generations; similarly, programs can be undertaken principally for the benefit of the current generation or they can be conducted mainly in the interest of future generations.

Essentially, the market discount rate in a perfectly competitive economy would be determined by the balance between individuals' time preferences[x] on the one hand, and the productivity of alternative investments on the other. Investments would continue to be undertaken so long as the rate of productivity for increments of investment is larger than the rate of preference for increments of present consumption to future consumption; the market discount rate would be determined by that rate which balances these two rates—that is, when the marginal rate of productivity is equal to the marginal rate of time preference.

Aside from the difficulties of measuring this (ideal) market rate or discount rate (which would be equal to the marginal rate of time preference and to the marginal rate of return on investments), and aside from the distortions of governmental action and of less than a perfectly competitive economy, some economists argue that the rate of time preference and the feelings of individuals with respect to the welfare of future versus current generations is affected by the opportunities for collective action. Stephen Marglin argues this position as follows:[15]

The objection to the market solution is that individuals may have preferences that, although an integral part of their attitudes toward consumption now versus consumption later, are inexpressible in the market place. In particular, none of us is able to put into effect in the market his preferences with regard to other people's consumption. I may well place less of a premium on my own consumption now as opposed to the consumption of an unknown member of a future generation at some specified date in the cooperative context of public investment, in which I know a sacrifice on my part will be matched by sacrifices by all other members of the community, than in an individualistic market arrangement in which I have no such assurance.

However, a discount rate which was determined to reflect the time preferences under these conditions of collective action, or a *social* rate of time preference (often called the social rate of discount), would be virtually impossible of measurement, and if used in the justification of *public* investments, would appear to have two unattractive features.[16] First, the use of different discount rates for the public and private sectors of the economy will not lead to the most efficient investment planning *from the standpoint of the economy and aside from matters of income distribution*. Second, there seems little doubt but that the use of a social rate of discount for public investments will result in an income transfer from a poorer current generation to a more well-to-do future

---

[x]That is, individuals' preferences with regard to substituting present consumption for future consumption.

generation (i.e., a regressive income redistribution).[17] (Obviously, it is well to ask whether the current generation would, in fact, have a social rate of discount which is less than the private or market rate of discount, if it was fully informed of the effects on economic efficiency and of the regressive income transfer.) Margolis (in reviewing the Eckstein and McKean books) summarizes some other views as well as the important issues as follows:[18]

Essentially Eckstein proposes as a discount rate, the rate at which the taxpayers privately value the funds which they provide, through taxation, to finance the project. He calls this rate the social cost of federal capital and he estimates it at 5 to 6 percent.[19] He defends this use of a private rate by urging that the agencies should accept the ethical judgment that consumers' sovereignty with regard to intertemporal choice should dominate. Therefore, a private rate of interest should be used in determining the choice of projects and the size of public investments.

Eckstein and Krutilla-Eckstein both recognize that in the political process the future is not valued solely in terms of the preferences of the current population; the beneficiaries should be future generations as well as the current one. But they use the time preferences of the current generation of taxpayers as the basis for the choice of a discount rate. *Actually there is no basis other than an arbitrary one upon which to select the particular generation or generations whose preferences should be regarded.* If, for example, we should select a later generation their preferences might be to keep the current generation at a minimum consumption level.

Though the economist cannot decide which generation's welfare should be maximized and therefore he cannot 'scientifically' choose a discount rate, he can be helpful in the selection of an appropriate social rate of time preference . . . In the specific area of water resources the economist can carry through the analysis at several rates, one of which would be Eckstein's social cost of federal capital and he can then inform the Congress of the time implications of the different rates. [Emphasis added.]

Another approach to estimation of the rate of social time preference was outlined in the 1961 report of Hufschmidt et al. to the Bureau of the Budget; this method calls for determining its value by ". . . discovering the marginal rate implicit in the Administration's goal of a certain rate of economic growth. This value judgment with respect to growth rate contains an implicit balancing at the margin of the Administration's time discount rate and social productivity of investment."[20] Significantly, though, the Panel of Consultants added the following qualification:[21]

One cannot really expect the Administration to hit upon a rate of growth regarded as optimal without much more knowledge of the economy's investment opportunities than we possess today. Thus the broad-brush targets of growth and investment rates which determine the marginal rate of time discount should themselves be revised in light of the marginal rate of discount implicit in them. In short, optimal rates of investment, growth, and marginal rate of discount are properly determined iteratively.

A second matter to be considered in the selection of an "appropriate" interest rate is that of risk, and a third is that of taxation.

Two aspects of risk (and uncertainty) must be accounted for.[22] These are: (1) the uncertainties of estimating accurately the future costs and benefits; and (2) risk aversion. While the uncertainties of cost and benefit prediction are often implicitly accounted for by increasing the discount rate over what it would be with no uncertainty (or risk), a more appropriate way of handling the problem would be to incorporate the uncertainties into the computation of the year-to-year estimates of cost and benefit, and to use the expected or most probable values. With uncertainties varying from year to year, and generally increasing over time, these adjustments should clearly be made year by year rather than on some arbitrary, constant, and increased interest-rate basis. Furthermore, this type of treatment will permit differentiation between uncertainties (or risks) and the time value of money, rather than combine the two aspects on some implicit and unidentifiable basis.

In addition to accounting for inaccuracies in estimating costs or benefits because of risk or uncertainty, it may also be necessary to make adjustments for "risk aversion," either in calculating the true market rate aside from "risk aversion," or in specifying a proper discount rate where "risk aversion" is preferable. Risk aversion applies to the preferences of individuals (or firms) with respect to undertaking investments with differing degrees of risk; some people, for example, are "risk averters" and are unwilling to invest in situations unless there is minimal or no risk (regardless of how high the expected return might be), while others or "risk takers" would hesitate to invest in situations unless there is at least some chance of a very large return (relative to the expected return), regardless of the risk.[23]

More specifically, risk averters generally would be unwilling to undertake investments unless the quoted return is higher than the expected return (or a so-called "risk aversion premium"), while risk takers might be willing to invest in situations having quoted returns less than the expected rate, if high returns were a reasonable possibility.[y]

The existence of these positive and negative "risk aversion" or "risk taking" premiums for individuals and firms within the private sector of the economy is emphasized mainly to indicate that investment analysts may find it necessary to make certain adjustments when viewing data obtained from the private sector. This is not to say, though, that the rate of discount used for evaluating public investments should reflect either an attitude of conservatism (or "risk aversion") or the reverse; in fact, it probably is more reasonable to take the position that public investments should be based simply on expected values and reflect neither risk aversion nor risk taking.[24]

[y]A simple example of the latter would be gamblers willing to place bets in a house crap game (e.g., on each roll of the die, those betting on "boxcars" or 12 receive a payoff of 30 to 1, thus producing a return which will fall below the expected value, since the probability of rolling a 12 is only 1 in 36).

Certainly, a related problem falling into the category of risk and uncertainty is that of overoptimism, particularly that as practiced by administrators or managers who do not bear the burdens of losses (should the revenues be lower or the costs higher than estimated, thus producing a loss—relative to the expected return).[25] Without question, such a situation has been common in the turnpike-revenue bond market as well as in other sectors of the transport industry. The extent to which overoptimistic estimates have been made, in some prominent cases, by engineering and financial consultants to turnpike authorities and underwriters can be surmised from the fact that: (1) interest rates on revenue bonds vary somewhat according to the general uncertainties and certainly with respect to state backing or support; and (2) the bond market has reacted to the overall aspects of uncertainty, risk aversion, and overoptimism by failing to consider toll projects unless they indicate a coverage factor (or the ratio of estimated revenues to estimated costs) of something in the order of 1.6.[z]

Two other aspects are important in determining an appropriate discount rate; they involve the dollar value (or matters of inflation or deflation) and taxation.

In situations of inflation or deflation, Hirshleifer, et al., recommend that all present and future costs and benefits be measured in constant dollars (rather than using either inflated or deflated dollar values) and that ". . . the discount rate should be adjusted to correspond to what would be the ruling rate if in fact people were confident that dollars would have constant purchasing power."[26] As a practical rule for adjusting the discount rate under current inflationary trends, they estimated that it would be appropriate to reduce the market discount rate by about 1/2 percent per annum, since the market rate probably reflects a built-in allowance for continuing inflation expectations. That is, when inflationary trends are expected to continue, the market discount rate is probably adjusted upwards to account for this. Thus, if market rates are used for application to analyses involving constant dollar values, they should be adjusted downward by the inflation-trend adjustment increment.

Federal, state, and local taxation directly affects the net or after-tax yield of private firms, and thus is of importance in determining the true productivity of incremental investment.[27] Foremost, it should be recognized that the private sector of the economy will tend to balance the marginal rate of time preference and the marginal rate of *after-tax* productivity (or marginal rate of *after-tax* return on investment), rather than the true or overall productivity (i.e., that before deducting tax payments); this result stems from federal, state, and local tax payments and deduction allowances, and will cause *underspending* in the private sector *if* we assume that taxes do *not* represent a proxy for costs of certain public services (such as fire and police protection) that were provided for the firms by government agencies. That is, if one accepts the assumption that

---

[z]Clearly, this can be and probably is a "chicken and egg" proposition; it is hardly certain which came first, or whether there is any dependent relationship between the coverage factor and the optimistic estimates.

taxes do *not* represent a *cost* associated with the private investments, then the yield or return of concern would be the before-tax return or overall productivity. Also, it would seem that the market solution caused by taxation policy (i.e., balance at the marginal rate of after-tax productivity) is probably not the best solution from a standpoint of economic efficiency, and will not directly permit determination of the marginal rate of before-tax productivity. Even so, Hirshleifer et al., attempted to estimate the marginal rate of productivity (and in so doing, to reflect the equity and debt relationships), and suggested that an appropriate figure for private utility investments[28] was in the range of 9 to 10 percent, after correction for taxation and inflation. However, if one should regard corporation income taxes as costs associated with the production of goods or services, the appropriate discount rate would be around 5 percent, according to the same authors.[29] As a concluding comment on recommendations for an "appropriate" discount rate for public investments, Hirshleifer, et al., say:[30]

Even for utility investments in the private sphere, we have seen that the capital market will supply funds only for projects promising (with the average degree of riskiness experienced in that sector) to yield around 9 or 10 percent. Unfortunately, public investment decision processes have on the whole a far worse record of overoptimism, so that the lowest discount rate for public projects we would recommend in practice, unless and until their record improves, is around 10 percent.

This view contrasts with that taken by the Panel of Consultants to the Bureau of the Budget, to wit:[31]

As a temporary expedient, in place of a social rate of time discount plus cutoff benefit-cost ratio, the Panel recommends that a rate synthesizing social time discount and opportunity cost be used. Pending a full-scale investigation by the Council of Economic Advisers of the value of the social rate of discount and the magnitude of opportunity costs, an interim rate of 4 to 5 percent would appear to be appropriate.

3

Demand Functions, Travel Benefits, and Travel Forecasting

Investment planning, benefit measurement, and travel forecasting all involve considerations of demand and they require analysis of the interactions among demand, cost, and pricing policies.

In this chapter, the problems of representing demand, and of characterizing the important interactions involving demand, will be discussed in some detail.

3.1 General Discussion of Demand Functions (or Demand Schedules) and Travel Benefits

A demand function is a statement of the dependent relationship between a desired quantity of tripmaking and the price of tripmaking (with price being the independent variable); that is, it describes either mathematically or graphically the number of trips which will be made at each level of trip price.[a] Of crucial importance, and unless noted otherwise, the trip price should be thought of as the overall payment in expense, time, and effort that a traveler *perceives or thinks about* in making a trip. The distinction between the *perceived* payment and the *actual* payment made by travelers is of importance and will be considered as it relates to investment planning. It should be emphasized that the *perceived* rather than actual trip price is appropriate for forecasting travel, since it is on this basis that the traveler makes decisions to travel or not, and to choose among various modes, routes, destinations, or times-of-day.

Figure 3-1 illustrates in simplest form[b] a demand curve for tripmaking between, say, a given set of origin and destination points, and for a specific time of day or common set of trip purposes. This demand curve holds only for a given level of income and population and for a certain pattern of land-use distribution, etc.[c] This is an aggregate demand curve, and it describes the volume or quantity of travel to be demanded at various prices for travelers having high and low incomes and for travelers having high and low urgencies for tripmaking. In other words, some people wanting to make trips between these points will value the

---

[a]A numerical tabulation of the demand function is often referred to as a "demand schedule," and a graphical display as a "demand curve."

[b]The demand curve is not necessarily, or probably, linear, but is shown in that form for the sake of simplicity.

[c]Another complication is involved; and that is, joint traveling or car pooling. Clearly, this consideration affects the output measure and is related in an important way both to cost and demand functions, even though it will be ignored in this discussion.

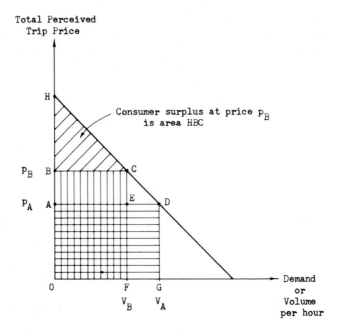

Figure 3-1. Simplified Demand Function.

trip differently simply because of differences in income and ability to pay for the trip, and others because of differences in the urgency of the trip or in the value of getting to their destination. In general, the demand curve will be downward sloping;[d] thus, as the price (or the combined travel effort, time, and expense) increases less trips will be made, everything else being equal, and if the price is reduced more trips will be made.

The proper specification of the unit of measurement for the quantity demanded or volume of tripmaking is particularly important and will be set identical to that used for the cost function (in order to simplify equilibration). As before, the measurement units for quantity demanded will be *q separate and different* vehicle trips per hour (desiring to move between a particular pair of zones and along a given facility); thus, as the price is lowered and the quantity demanded increases, additional *new* vehicle tripmakers will be traveling, rather than former travelers making more frequent use of the facility. (Other terms such as "trips," "travelers," "tripmakers," or "tripmaking" are all intended to correspond to the above definition and description.) However, it is also

---

[d]Traditionally, for graphical illustrations, the independent and dependent variable axes are reversed for the demand curve; the dependent variable is shown on the *x*-axis and the independent variable on the *y*-axis.

important to note that this specification of measurement units implies that each vehicle trip will involve an equal number of passengers (that is, identical car pooling).

The demand function may also be interpreted and used to indicate the willingness of vehicle tripmakers to pay for travel, and thus to provide measures of the *value or benefit* associated with particular trips. However, some distinctions are necessary with regard to the latter point. For one, we must distinguish between what tripmakers actually *do* "pay" and what they are *willing* to "pay." For example, if the price were p_B (see Figure 3-1) and if V_B trips an hour were made, the value of the trip *for the V_Bth tripmaker or the tripmaker at the "margin"* can be determined; that is, the marginal tripmaker or person having the lowest trip value among those traveling just broke even, paying exactly as much as the trip was worth to him.[e] Obviously, this same value also serves as a measure of the amount each of the other travelers *does* pay, as distinct from the total amount that the others would be *willing* to pay. No more than V_B trips would be made, because the fixed price (p_B) is higher to those not making the trip than its value to them; thus, for price p_B, those not making the trip would find that their position on the demand curve is to the right of and below point C.

At this point, a digression is necessary, as it is important to distinguish more precisely between "benefit" (and "user cost") as commonly defined by the highway engineer and that as used by the economist, the latter practice being followed in this text. *These distinctions are key to a full understanding of all that follows.*

First, the economist (usually) defines *benefit* as being equivalent to the trip value or to the gross amount that travelers would be willing to pay for a trip.[f] Referring to Figure 3-1, if the price were at a level p_B, travelers would be willing to pay amounts as indicated by the demand curve to the left of point C; or, more specifically, if the price were p_B, then the total benefit or value accruing to the V_B tripmakers would be equal to area *HOFC* or the entire area under the demand curve and to the left of point C. If the price were lowered to p_A, then the total benefit or value accruing to V_A tripmakers would be equal to area *HOGD*.

Second, the highway engineers' definition of "benefit" does not correspond to the economists' definition, but (for the former) is usually defined as the reduction in user cost which accompanies a price change (where price is construed broadly in terms of the time, effort, and expense of travel). In this

---

[e]A uniform single price has been assumed, and matters concerning heterogeneity and interpersonal comparisons are largely ignored.

[f]This is not to say, however, that all of this gross benefit should be included in the totals used to justify public investments; this is, in part, a matter of judgment and will be discussed later in the section and in Chapter 5.

example, if the price were at a level of p_B, then the "cost" *to each user*[g] would be the same as the price he pays or p_B. (Of course, all but the tripmaker at the margin would be willing to pay more than that amount.) If the price were dropped to p_A, then the "user cost" would drop accordingly. The difference in "user cost," or reduction from p_B to p_A, is what the engineer usually defines as the "benefit" per trip. Thus, the total amount of "user cost reduction" or total amount of "benefit" associated with a price reduction from p_B to p_A—as usually defined by the highway engineer—would be equal to the area *BADC*. Throughout this text, however, the economists' definition of benefit will be adopted, in which case "benefit" as defined by the highway engineer more properly should be called the *change in total net user benefit* stemming from a price change. (More than anything else, and so long as one is interested in gross benefit while including consumer surplus, this is simply a change in terminology.)

Returning to the main discussion, for all tripmakers other than the one at the "margin," it is reasonable to expect that they receive or accrue some value or benefit *over and above* the price they do pay. In the terms of the economist, all tripmakers or consumers except the traveler at the margin would accrue a surplus. Put differently, an individual will *usually* be willing to pay a little more than he is actually charged or than he does pay in time, effort, and expense; consequently, he usually will receive a little *extra* value or net benefit. This surplus or *additional* value or benefit (over and above the price paid) is termed *consumer's surplus* by the economist.

It is reasonably evident that in making specific trips, most travelers are willing to pay more than the short-run loss of travel time, discomfort and inconvenience, and out-of-pocket expense which are required (if these are the only expenditures they consider). The short-run payments serve to indicate their perceived user travel benefit, other than for any consumer surpluses. Also, over the long-run, they are willing to pay for vehicle ownership, operation, maintenance and repair, vehicle accident insurance premiums, and vehicle garaging, *all of these to the extent that they may not already be included in the short-run perceived travel price.* However, when travelers *in the short-run* do perceive all these actual payments while making decisions about specific trips, no distinction is necessary between short-run and long-run user payments and benefits; should they be different, though, the distinction will be important and will be necessary in order to properly determine user benefits. On the other hand, travel forecasting or the determination of the actual tripmaking volume (i.e., equilibrium flow) will depend solely on short-run considerations, whether travelers include only out-of-pocket payments or whether they account for total or long-run expenditures in making short-run tripmaking decisions.

The specific details of accounting for these distinctions and different situations will be covered in the following section.

---

[g]There is no necessary relationship between (real) cost to society and "cost" to the user; so no confusion will develop, the latter is placed within quotation marks.

3.2 Determination of Actual Quantity Demanded or
Equilibrium Flow and of Travel Benefits: An Introduction

The quantity of tripmaking which will be demanded (that is, the equilibrium flow) must be jointly determined from price-volume[h] and demand functions. More simply, equilibrium flow will be determined by the interaction of demand functions (which define the quantity of tripmaking at each price level), on the one hand, and of price-volume functions (which describe the prices which will face the tripmaker at different volumes or levels of tripmaking), on the other.

Since we are concerned both with the problem of determining the most efficient investment policy and with that of determining the actual or equilibrium flow, failure on the part of travelers to account for all private travel payments (that is, payments which they do make but do not consider) in their short-run tripmaking calculus would necessitate use of two sets of price-volume and demand functions, one to account for the circumstances as they are perceived, and the second as they actually are. However, throughout this analysis, it will be assumed that the (privately) *perceived* payments, *aside from tolls* (or other similar charges), are exactly equivalent to the *actual* total private payments and are equal to the average variable costs as described in Chapter 2, equation (2-15).[1] (This implicitly assumes that when making short-run trip decisions travelers account for all vehicle ownership, vehicle operation, parking, garaging, accident and facility repair and maintenance *costs* etc.—the last as represented by uniform user taxes—and that these variable *costs* are just equal to the perceived payments on the part of travelers.) These perceived payments are the total payments (or private costs to the user, as he views them) *before* any tolls or other charges are imposed (and which will be regarded as being directly perceived).

At the outset, the distinction between *price* and *cost* and between *price-volume functions* and *cost functions*, as used in this discussion, must be clearly understood.[i] As defined and described in Chapter 2, the total human and material resources required or forfeited by the public at large to provide for a certain quantity of tripmaking are the costs; the price, on the other hand, refers to the privately perceived payment (i.e., *user* "cost") which travelers must make (in both money and nonmoney terms) if they are to be provided with a certain quantity of trips. Also, the cost functions describe the dependent relationship

---

[h]Price-volume functions as used herein will refer to the private or user "cost" function which is perceived by tripmakers; in short, it may be thought of as the "user cost" function or "price-volume" function which is faced by tripmakers. Those acquainted with the economics (theory of the firm) literature should not confuse this definition or usage of "price-volume" functions with the usual industry supply curve.

[i]Again, attention is called to the fact that usage of these terms is very different from that used (in "theory of the firm" economics) to describe and determine cost and supply conditions for firms under perfect competition.

between public cost and quantity of tripmaking (the latter being the independent variable), while the price-volume functions represent the relationship between price (or privately perceived payment or user "cost") and the quantity of tripmaking. Price and cost may or may not be directly related, and may or may not be equal, depending on the pricing policy (among other matters); the possibilities in this regard will be discussed thoroughly in later sections.

Determination of equilibrium flow, or the actual volume use which a facility *will* experience (and of the benefit or value which will actually accrue to its users, as well as the ultimate costs of providing the transport service), depends on a joint consideration of price-volume functions and demand curves. Thus, it is necessary that the price-volume curve and demand curve have dependent and independent variables which are stated on a commensurate scale; for example, the unit price which different numbers of travelers will have to pay for using a particular facility (as shown by the price-volume curve) must be stated in the same overall units as the price which different numbers of travelers will be willing to pay (as shown by the demand curve). Of equal importance, the price scale for the demand curve, and thus for the price-volume curve as well, must be stated in *perceived* rather than actual payments by the traveler, where the two differ. Again, those money payments which the traveler or user pays over the longer run but which he *does not consider* in making *short-run* travel choices are not included in the price scale of the demand schedule. Similarly, there must be a correspondence between the output units for the price-volume and demand functions, which in this case will be vehicle trips per hour moving between a common set of origins and destinations (which are separated by distance d). Further, only passenger-carrying private automobiles are appropriate for this one-dimensional analysis of cost and demand and of the interaction between price-volume and demand functions. (If a mixed stream of goods and passenger vehicles of different types were used, the cost functions would have to be formulated in terms of the volume of each type, and would have to be related to demand functions for each type of vehicle trip with all cross relations being accounted for. To include these less simplified conditions would complicate this presentation to the point of blurring the framework and methodology.) Restriction to passenger carrying vehicles will simplify greatly the construction of suitable cost and price-volume functions, but suggests the necessity of adding another dimension to the demand functions. Specifically, with the output measure in vehicle trips for both price-volume and demand functions, it is implicitly assumed that the number of passengers per vehicle remains constant for all trips made during the hour.

There can be no question that this last assumption is unrealistic and that the number of passengers per vehicle trip varies from hour to hour, from one income level to another, from person to person, and thus from year to year as incomes and preferences change. More appropriate treatment of this matter would extend far beyond the simple analysis attempted here. (Further discussion of this point will be included when the development of intratemporal or hour-to-hour demand functions is accomplished.)

To illustrate in a general way the interaction between price-volume and demand functions and to indicate equilibrium conditions, consider the price-volume and demand conditions *as they presently exist for most public highways*, and are portrayed in Figure 3-2 for facility x; essentially, it is assumed that the price-volume function is equivalent to the short-run average variable cost function[j] or $sravc_x(q)$ in Figure 3-2, and that demand is stable or constant from hour to hour and can be represented by only one hourly demand function. (This implies that demand does not fluctuate either hour-to-hour or year-to-year and that our pricing policy is such that both prices and the price-volume function are not dependent on the marginal costs of transport service or on the total costs of the service. Also, for the moment, we will consider only the short-run equilibrium conditions and leave till later an exploration of the consequences of system expansion or contraction.) For this simplified case, the actual or equilibrium flow will be q_0 and the equilibrium price will be p_0. That the flow and price will stabilize at (approximately) this level can be seen by assuming a different level of flow and considering the consequences. If the flow were q_1, for example, the resultant user price would be p_1, as seen from the price-volume curve, $sravc_x(q)$; but if the price were p_1, only q_2 travelers would be willing to make that payment and to travel. And, in turn, a flow of only q_2 would require

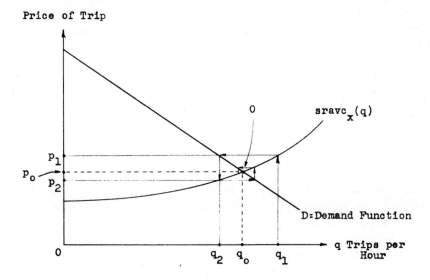

Figure 3-2. Simplified Equilibrium Relationships.

[j]Also, recall that tripmakers are assumed to be homogeneous with respect to privately perceived user "costs."

a payment of only p_2, a price which will cause a travel flow above q_0 but below q_1. Iterations will continue in such a cobweb fashion[k] until a price and flow level is determined which will be consistent with both the price-volume and demand functions.

These equilibrium flow conditions imply that travelers having a *trip value* which is less than the required payment p_0 (i.e., those travelers whose position on the demand curve is to the right of and below point "0") will not travel, while all those with trip values equal to or above p_0 will make the trip. Obviously, travel benefit accrues only to those who *do* travel and is equal to the area under the demand curve and to the left of point "0"; note that this is the *total* benefit accruing to travelers rather than the *net* travel benefit, where net benefit would be defined as the difference between total benefits and total payment and is equal to the total consumers' surpluses. (More accurately, this would include only the perceived travel benefit unless travelers perceived all actual payments.) Finally, note that the traveler *at the margin* or q_0th traveler, whose benefit or value (as described by the demand function) is just equal to his payment, accrues no consumer surplus or net benefit.

3.3 Intratemporal and Intertemporal Demand Relationships

During a given time period or, say, during a year, demand may fluctuate dramatically from hour to hour, from day to day, or from season to season. These intratemporal demand fluctuations produce the peak-load situations which commonly result in traffic congestion and which (together with inter-temporal fluctuations) add greatly to the complications of determining equilibrium flow and price levels. Yet their proper consideration is of key importance to investment planning, to pricing, and to the efficient utilization of facilities.

Part (a) of Figure 3-3 illustrates (hypothetical) demand functions for 3 different hours of the day and their interaction with the price-volume function; if the demand functions for all 24 hours were plotted, the quantity demanded versus time-of-day results would probably be somewhat as shown in part (b).

First, different demand functions for different times-of-day have been hypothesized to reflect differences in trip value for various trip purposes or preferred times of travel. For example, it would appear reasonable to argue that work trips are more valuable and urgent than shopping trips, and that they are somewhat restricted with respect to the times of day at which they can be made. Second, though no attempt will be made to handle the problem within this discussion, it should be pointed out that these hourly demand functions are interdependent or have cross-relations. That is, the tripmaking during hour H_1 is partially dependent on the *equilibrium* flow conditions, and thus demand

---

[k]However, it should be noted that not all price-volume and demand relationships will cause a "cobweb" type of convergence on the equilibrium point, as shown here.

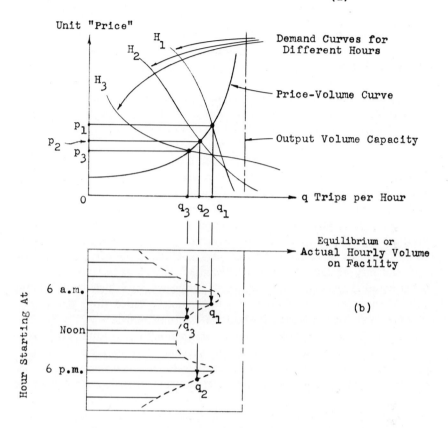

(a)

Unit "Price"

H_1

H_2

H_3

Demand Curves for Different Hours

Price-Volume Curve

P_1

P_2

P_3

Output Volume Capacity

0

q Trips per Hour

q_3 q_2 q_1

Equilibrium or Actual Hourly Volume on Facility

6 a.m.

Noon

6 p.m.

q_1

q_3

q_2

(b)

Hour Starting At

NOTE: For simplicity, demand curves for only three hours are shown. Also, for demand functions the dependent and independent variable axes have been reversed.

Figure 3-3. Short-Term Intratemporal Demand and Price-Volume Relationships.

functions, during the other hours of the day, and vice versa. Or put in practical terms, the exact time of the home-to-work trip depends not only on the trip price and value of reporting to work exactly on time, but also on the trip prices and values of going to work somewhat earlier (and avoiding congestion, say) or somewhat later (and avoiding congestion but getting one's pay docked); similarly, the evening-out-to-dinner trips and shopping trips depend not only on the trip price and trip value of traveling during the most "suitable" hour but also on those during earlier or later hours. These cross-relation (or cross-elasticity) problems clearly cannot be ignored in any realistic study, just as those with respect to *modal cross-relations* cannot be overlooked in any full analysis.[2] (That is, as conditions get better or worse on one mode, they affect not only the absolute amount of tripmaking but switches from or to other modes as well.) A first approximation of the models which account for these cross-relations is included in Appendix 2.

Also, each hourly demand function implicitly embodies the number of passengers per vehicle making vehicle trips during that hour, and it is implied that this ridership factor is constant throughout the hour and from vehicle to vehicle. Clearly, this oversimplifies, and for a more accurate analysis it would be necessary to dimension each of the hourly demand functions by the number of passengers per vehicle and to represent the cross-relations between all sets of demand functions. For example, work trips and social-recreational vehicle trips vary widely in terms of the number of passengers per vehicle and are affected quite differently with respect to this variable; for the former, an increase in passengers significantly adds to the discomfort and inconvenience of the work trip (both to and from home), as well as to the overall travel time, while for the latter, an increase in passengers per car may add little to the trip costs (for most trips) and may actually increase the pleasure.[3] These aspects, plus others of a similar nature, suggest that the number of passengers per vehicle implicit in the hourly demand functions should, at a minimum, be varied from year to year according to changes in income levels or preference patterns.

Shifts in demand from time period to time period (or say, from year to year) or intertemporal demand fluctuations can be handled by utilization of a separate set of intratemporal or hourly demand functions for each demand period or each year. However, to simplify the graphics, let us assume that we can represent the set of hourly demand functions (as shown in Figure 3-3) for each year by some sort of aggregate or averaged demand function; in this case, year to year or intertemporal demand fluctuations would be as shown in Figure 3-4. The shift of the demand function upward and to the right implies that population growth, or shifts in land-use, or shifts in consumer preference patterns, or income growth, etc., would singly or in combination produce increases in demand.[1] For the hypothetical demand-curve shifts and price-volume curve shown in Figure 3-4, it is evident that the actual quantity demanded or equilibrium flow during the early years, increases faster than during later years (in both absolute and relative terms); such a result would be the usual result for *uniform* increases in demand and for facilities or systems whose capacity remains fixed over the years. Also, if the price-volume curve were vertical in the region of equilibrium, then no increases in actual quantity demanded or equilibrium flow would occur.

---

[1]Shifts in demand (that is, shifts of the demand function) do *not necessarily* mean that shifts in the quantity demanded or equilibrium flow (or volume actually using facility) *will* occur.

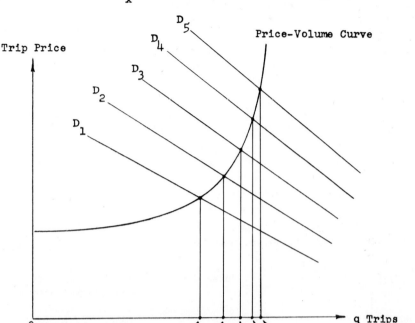

Figure 3-4. Intertemporal Demand and Price-Volume Relationships.

3.4 Equilibrium Flow and Benefit Conditions for Facilities of Varying Levels of Capacity (or Service)

To illustrate the changes in actual quantity demanded or equilibrium flow[m] that accompany changes in facility capacity (or service capability) for a single time period, the relationships shown in Figure 3-5 will be helpful. As before, let us restrict our attention to approximately the same situation which exists today for public highways, while assuming that the price-volume function and average variable cost functions are equivalent and that all payments by travelers are perceived in the course of their tripmaking. (For this case, it should be easy to

---

[m]Note that a change or increase in flow or volume of movement is *not* called an increase in demand (which implies a shift in the demand function); a drop in the price which induces an increase in the quantity demanded or equilibrium flow is just that, and *not an increase in demand*!

convince one that highway improvements will virtually always lower the price-volume function or translate it horizontally and to the right as shown in Figure 3-5.) As such, improvement of facility A to the level of B will drop the equilibrium travel price from p_A to p_B and will induce more tripmaking; that is, the quantity of travel demanded will increase from a volume of V_A to V_B. It may be helpful (for the traffic or highway engineer) to point out that the volume V_A which formerly used facility A, and now uses facility B, may be regarded as the "diverted volume," and that the increase in volume or tripmaking may be termed the "induced" or "generated" volume.

As for the travel benefits associated with these two facilities, and the implied pricing policy, they can be determined in the fashion suggested earlier. For facility A, and its equilibrium flow and price levels of V_A and p_A, respectively, the *total* travel benefit (for V_A trips) would be equal to area $AFOC$, while that for facility B (and V_B trips) would be equal to area $BGOC$. The *additional* or *incremental* benefit accruing to travelers from the improvement would be equal to the difference between the total benefit for B and that for A, or would be equal to area $ABGF$. Also, the *net* benefit (or difference between

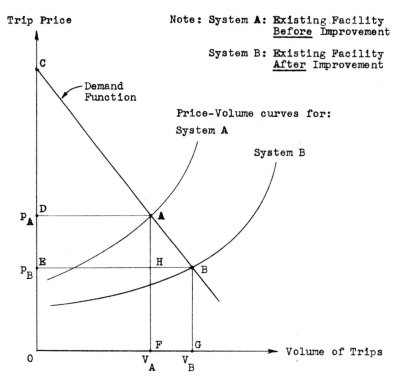

Figure 3-5. Equilibrium Conditions for Different Facilities.

total user or traveler benefit and user payments) before improvement would be equal to area *ADC* and after improvement would be area *BEC*. The difference between these two totals, or the change in net travel benefit, would be equal to area *ABED*.[n]

Also, it is well to note that those who traveled both before and after improvement accrue a larger increment in net benefit than do the new or induced travelers.[o] Specifically, each traveler among the volume V_A will experience a net benefit increase of p_A minus p_B from the improvement, and as a group will find their net benefit increased by *AHED*; by contrast, the first additional or new traveler will receive a net benefit (from improvement) that is slightly less, and the last additional traveler (that is, the V_Bth traveler) or traveler at the margin will receive no net benefit. The induced travelers $(V_B - V_A)$ will each receive a net benefit that averages $1/2(p_A - p_B)$, assuming that the demand curve is linear; as a group, their net benefit will be equal to the triangle *ABH*.

The above point is emphasized, since highway engineers often attribute the entire unit increase in net benefit (of p_A minus p_B) to both the former *and* induced travelers, a practice which is incorrect and which will overstate the increase *unless* the demand happens to be perfectly inelastic.[p] This case, that of perfectly inelastic demand, is illustrated in Figure 3-6. Such a case appears to be unrealistic, but nevertheless is commonly made (though implicitly) by highway engineers in many, if not most, engineering economy studies.[4] While engineers do not explicitly assume or determine that the demand is perfectly inelastic, it is the practical result of assuming that the equilibrium flow or actual volume usage after improvement will be identical to the volume before improvement.

Turning now to the longer-term effects of shifts in demand, as related to changes in facility capacity and/or service, these can be determined from the curves in Figure 3-7. (In this situation, the comparative relationships are shown from the *end* of year 0 through the end of year 5. Also, let us ignore the circumstances while facility *A* would be in the process of being improved to the level of facility *B*.) The year by year equilibrium conditions can be determined for the two alternatives, as well as the benefit and net benefit circumstances. Also, the functions shown in Figure 3-7 can be used to describe the increases in traffic flow and to relate these increases to the move usual terminology of the engineer. Specifically, if facility *A* were improved to the level of *B* and opened for usage at the end of year 0, the volume which would have used facility

---

[n]This change in net travel benefit from improvement is what highway engineers generally define as "benefit" from improvement.

[o]This involves a rather heroic assumption regarding the interpersonal relationships among travelers.

[p]The elasticity of demand is defined as the percentage change in quantity demanded that results from a one-percent change in the price. Perfect inelasticity would occur when the elasticity of demand is equal to zero for all price changes; thus, a price reduction would not increase the amount of tripmaking.

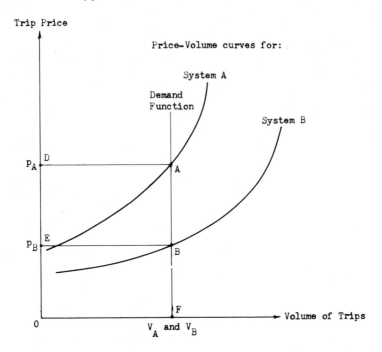

Figure 3-6. Equilibrium Conditions for Perfectly Inelastic Demand.

A (had it not been improved) or $V_{A,0}$ is diverted to facility B; this volume or $V_{A,0}$ would be the so-called "diverted traffic."[q] An additional volume of traffic will be induced to travel because of the improved service conditions (as measured by the drop in equilibrium price); this increment of volume will be equal to $V_{B,0}$ minus $V_{A,0}$ and is equivalent to the so-called "induced volume." The additional increases in traffic flow from year to year (that is, following the end of year 0) can be regarded as the normal traffic growth for facility B; during the first full year, the normal traffic growth for B would be $V_{B,1}$ minus $V_{B,0}$, while the increased flow from the end of the year 0 to the end of year 5 or $V_{B,5}$ minus $V_{B,0}$ is the normal traffic growth during the first five years for facility B.

---

[q]Strictly speaking, it may be more correct to describe this component of volume (or $V_{A,O}$) as the "base" or "current" traffic. However, if facility or system B represents a replacement for system A (the latter of which is then abandoned), and if facility B is on new location but between the same pair of origin and destination points, then one might describe this component as diverted traffic. Since these definitional distinctions are not crucial to this exposition, the latter usage will be adopted for convenience.

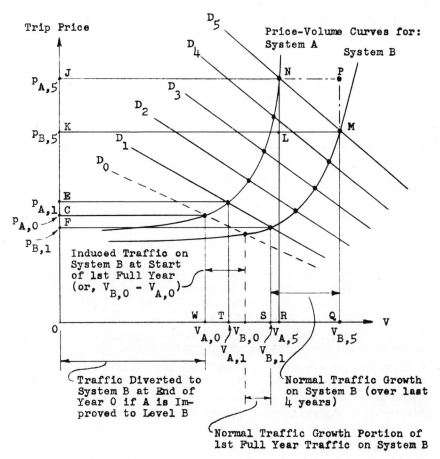

Figure 3-7. Equilibrium Conditions (by Year) for Unimproved and Improved System or Facility.

3.5 Joint Determination of Equilibrium Flow, Price, and Toll for Certain Interdependent Cost, Price and Intratemporal Demand Functions: An Example Problem

Thus far, most of the discussion has dealt with conditions on public highways under existing pricing policies; in these situations, it is reasonable to regard the price to the traveler during hour h as being functionally related to the facility capacity and to the demand for travel only during hour h. That is, the equilibrium price in no way is affected by the demand or equilibrium flow during other hours of travel. However, with some pricing policies and even while overlooking intratemporal demand *cross*-elasticities,[5] the price to travelers during hour h can be directly affected by the demand during the other hours of travel. In some of these cases, the determination of equilibrium flow and price will not be so straightforward or simple as were the preceding cases, but will require the use of more complex analytical or computational techniques.

To illustrate some of the difficulties which can arise and one possibly way to account for the interdependencies, an example will be included which is applicable to toll facilities as normally operated and priced. The resultant linear programming model might be described as a *quasi* nonlinear toll pricing program.

The problem *as usually viewed by the toll authority* is to determine the uniform toll rate which will provide sufficient revenues (net of the facility operating and maintenance expenses) to just cover the bond payments or capital plus interest costs for the facility. Stated in this fashion, the toll rate will not include the variable facility costs for maintenance and operation (M & O) expenses; these are excluded from the computations for the toll rate simply for the sake of convenience. They are included as part of the average variable costs which are perceived by travelers and they are assumed to vary directly and linearly with the usage of the facility. Also, the toll authority's criterion for setting the toll rate (or objective function) may be restated in either of two equivalent ways: (1) Find the lowest rate which provides sufficient revenues (net of M & O costs) to cover bond payments; or (2) Find the rate which provides sufficient revenues and which maximizes usage of the facility. Such an objective function is not argued to be the best one for either the bondholders or the general public, but is adopted to be generally consistent with the practices of most toll authorities and for use in this illustrative example.

For the above, the toll pricing policy amounts to average cost pricing *for the fixed facility expenditures* (or, generally, capital plus interest charges), in which the fixed facility costs are spread uniformly among the total daily volume of tripmakers. It can be assumed that the remainder of the total user price (or total price minus toll) is equal to the short-run average variable cost. Thus, while the *toll* will not vary from hour to hour (or from demand period to demand period), the average variable cost portion of the total price will vary to the extent that demand functions vary intratemporally. With tolls being dependent upon the facility costs and daily flow, the latter of which simultaneously depends upon the intratemporal demand functions as they interact with the average variable cost function and toll level, it can be seen that a complex set of interdependencies and mathematical relationships will be required for the determination of the toll which maximizes flow and covers the fixed facility costs.

The interrelationships can be stated most simply in mathematical form and will consist of three parts: (1) the intratemporal demand functions, in which the quantity demanded during the ith hour is a function of the facility toll and the other perceived payments for the time, effort, and expense of travel during the *i*th hour; (2) the user price-volume functions for tolls and "other perceived payments," in which price is a function of the facility toll and the quantity demanded during the *i*th hour; and (3) the roadway toll function, in which the toll is a function of the total daily flow[r] and the fixed facility costs. Mathematically,

$$q_i = f(p_i) \qquad\qquad , \text{ for } i = 1, \ldots, 24 \qquad\qquad (3\text{-}1)$$

$$p_i = f(q_i, t) \qquad\qquad , \text{ for } i = 1, \ldots, 24 \qquad\qquad (3\text{-}2)$$

and

$$t = f(F_x, q_1, q_2, \ldots, q_{24}) \quad , \qquad\qquad (3\text{-}3)$$

where q_i is the quantity demanded or equilibrium flow during the *i*th hour, p_i is the price per trip (toll plus other perceived payments) during the *i*th hour, t is the uniform toll per trip charged during all hours, and F_x is the fixed cost for facility x. (For the linear programming formulation of this problem, the variable facility costs will be included in "other perceived payments"; thus the toll as calculated will only include the fixed cost portion of the facility costs. The equilibrium flow and price levels will be unaffected by this manipulation, however, so long as the variable facility costs vary directly and linearly with volume.)

While precise mathematical expressions for user price-volume and roadway toll functions would be nonlinear, they can be approximated by using a series of linear expressions for their representation; demand functions will be assumed to be linear. The linear forms (or linearizations) for demand, price-volume, and toll functions, respectively, might be stated as follows:[s]

$$q_i = a_i - b_i p_i \qquad\qquad , \text{ for } i = 1, \ldots, 24 \qquad\qquad (3\text{-}4)$$

$$p_i \geqslant c_j + d_j q_i + t \qquad\begin{array}{l} \text{for } i = 1, \ldots, 24 \\ \text{, for } j = 1, \ldots, m \end{array} \qquad (3\text{-}5)$$

---

[r]For convenience, daily rather than annual volumes will be used; thus, it is assumed that each day during the year has identical demand conditions.

[s]If the hour-to-hour demand *cross*-relations (i.e., the fact that the demand for travel during the *i*th hour is dependent not only upon the price p_i during the *i*th hour, but is also dependent upon the prices during all other hours of the day) are also accounted for, then equation (3-4) would become:

$$q_i = a_i - b_1 p_1 - \cdots - b_i p_i - \cdots - b_{24} p_{24} \, , for \; i = 1, \ldots, 24.$$

Again, for a fuller discussion of this more complete formulation, and some illustrative results, see: Wohl, 1970, pp. 208-214 (Case 2).

$$t \geqslant f_e - g_e \sum_{i=1}^{24} q_i \quad , \text{ for } e = 1, \ldots, n \qquad (3\text{-}6)$$

where a_i and b_i are the demand coefficients during the ith hour, c_j and d_j are the cost coefficients for the jth user price-volume linearization, and f_e and g_e are the cost coefficients for the eth facility (fixed) cost linearization.

In some cases, the demand during certain hours of the day will be identical (or virtually so), and thus one demand function can be used for the flow conditions during more than one hour, reducing the calculations. In such an instance, q_i will represent the *hourly* flow or quantity demanded during each hour of the ith demand period, where the ith demand period would include k_i hours where there are r separate demand periods. Then equation (3-6) would become:

$$t \geqslant f_e - g_e \sum_{i=1}^{r} (k_i)(q_i) \quad . \qquad (3\text{-}7)$$

Then, for equations (3-4) and (3-5), $i = 1, \ldots, r$.

To apply the linear programming formulation shown above in equations (3-4), (3-5), and (3-7) to a specific toll facility, it will be necessary to determine the appropriate demand and average variable cost (or price-volume) functions for the particular situation, in addition to the facility costs, and then to linearize these cost functions (and demand functions if they are nonlinear) for use in the linear program. For the illustrative example to follow, the linear and nonlinear representations of the demand, price-volume (less toll), and toll functions will be assumed to be as shown in Figures 3-8, 3-9, and 3-10; the cost and demand coefficients embodied in those curves and in the accompanying mathematical expressions were not developed from specific field data pertaining to a particular situation, but represent hypothesized conditions which were judged to be somewhat typical of a fairly large class of four-lane, high volume, and high cost through-traffic highway facilities.[6]

To provide some insight regarding the facility costs, as well as the travel speeds and user travel prices (less toll), the following data and that shown in Table 3-1 will be helpful. First, fixed facility costs (that is, the costs that do not vary with output or volume levels) for the 5-mile four-lane facility included construction costs of $1.1 million per mile (with a replacement life of 40 years), right-of-way costs of $0.354 million per mile (with an indefinite life), and certain fixed annual maintenance and administrative costs of $31,600 per mile. Placed on an annual cash-flow payment basis,[t] these fixed costs will be $125,946 per mile per year, and converted to a daily basis will be $1,725 for the entire

---

[t]The capital outlays can be converted to an annual cash flow payment basis by using capital recovery factors as shown in equation (2-12).

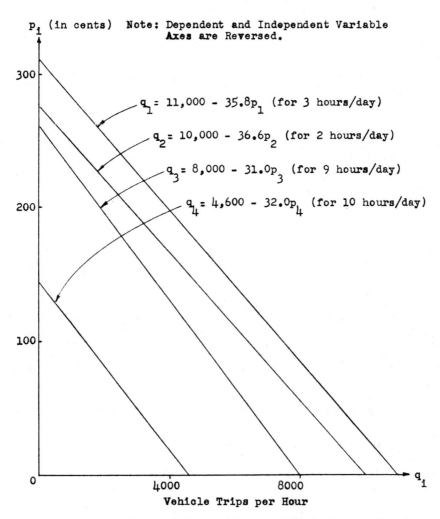

Figure 3-8. Hourly Traffic Demand During All Daily Demand Periods Versus User Travel Price for 5-Mile Trip.

five-mile facility; this latter figure is comparable with that shown in Figure 3-10 for *ARC*. Second, the average variable costs or user travel prices (less toll) were assumed to be as shown in Figure 3-9 and to rise gradually, but at ever increasing rates, from about 12 cents per vehicle-mile (or 60 cents per 5-mile vehicle trip). The resultant travel speeds and user travel prices (less toll) for various volume levels and for this four-lane facility would be as shown in Table 3-1.

Using these illustrative cost and demand data, this toll pricing problem was

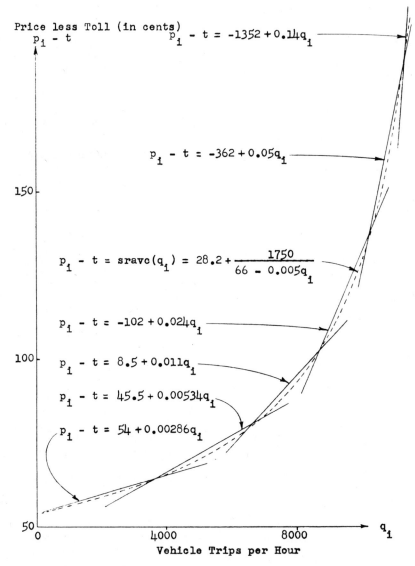

Figure 3-9. Linearizations of Average Variable Cost Function for 5-Mile Trips.

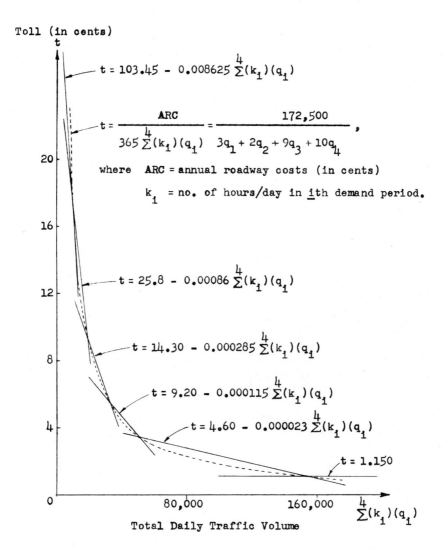

Figure 3-10. Linearizations of Average Toll Versus Daily Traffic Volume Relationship for 5-Mile Road.

programmed, using a linear programming formulation, and run on an IBM electronic computer; also, a run was made for a second set of coefficients which were identical to the first set, other than for the demand intercept, a_i, which was reduced by one-half.[u] The appropriate objective function necessary to bring about equilibrium and produce sufficient revenues to

---

[u]The LP formulation and tableau for the first computer run (that is, for the first set of coefficients) are shown in Appendixes 3 and 4.

Table 3-1
Speed and User Travel Prices (Less Toll) for Hypothesized Four-Lane Facility

Average Volume Level in Vehicles per lane-hour*	Average Speed in m.p.h.	Average User Travel Price (Less Toll), in Cents per Vehicle-mile
500	56 m.p.h.	11.8 ¢/vehicle-mile
1000	46	13.2
1500	36	15.4
2000	26	19.2

*The volume figures on the abscissa of Figure 3-9 are those for all four lanes and thus four times these figures.

cover the fixed facility costs would be maximization of the total daily volume, subject to nonnegativity restrictions[v] and to the demand, price-volume, and roadway toll constraints. The results for these computer runs as shown in Table 3-2.

In the first run, it is evident that the toll represents only a small portion of

Table 3-2
Results from Linear Programming (LP)

	Toll Pricing Model			
	LP Results for:			
Variable		Run 1	Run 2	Description of Units
(Objective)	z	112,726	35,998	*Daily* vehicle trips
(Toll)	t	2.01¢	5.06¢	Toll per 5-mile trip
(Price During ith Demand Period)	p_1	94.4¢	68.0¢	Price per 5-mile trip during the ith demand period
	p_2	85.9	66.5	
	p_3	77.2	64.8	
	p_4	63.5	60.2	
(Hourly Flow During ith Demand Period)	q_1	7622	3067	Trips per *hour* for 3 hours
	q_2	6855	2566	Trips per *hour* for 2 hours
	q_3	5606	1990	Trips per *hour* for 9 hours
	q_4	2569	375	Trips per *hour* for 10 hours

[v]By nonnegativity restrictions, the variables $(q_i, p_i$ and $t)$ are restricted to nonnegative values (i.e., values $\geqslant 0$). The objective function is:

$$\text{Maximize } z = \sum_{i=1}^{r} (k_i)(q_i) \quad.$$

the total user price for peak-period travelers and has little effect upon the resultant flow; in essence, congestion tends to control the volume level. This is particularly evident when one compares the price and volume levels for the 1st and 4th demand periods, wherein the latter suffers little from the effects of congestion. Notice, though, that travelers during the 4th demand period are much more sensitive to changes in demand (or, for that matter, changes in roadway costs or congestion) than are travelers during the 1st or 2nd demand periods. For example, when the demand intercept was reduced by one-half for *all* demand periods for run 2, the resultant volume was reduced by 60 percent for the 1st demand period but by 85 percent for the 4th demand period; alternatively, it can be shown that demand during the 4th period is much less inelastic than that during the 1st period.

For the first set of demand data, changes in roadway costs would only result in small changes in both tolls and volume levels, since demand during all periods is inelastic. For the second set, more substantial changes would result, as demand during the 3rd and 4th periods is highly elastic and that during the first two periods is only slightly inelastic.

Another point of interest regards the extent to which error is introduced by the linear approximations to the roadway toll and user price-volume functions. Briefly, a visual examination of the latter curves in Figure 3-9 warrants the conclusion that little error is introduced in user prices so long as hourly volumes in any demand period are below the 10,000 level. However, with respect to errors introduced by the roadway toll linear approximation, two aspects are of interest.

First, it should be evident from an examination of Figure 3-10 and from joint consideration of the demand and user price functions that discrepancies in toll rates affect the resultant flow levels only to a negligible extent, so long as the total daily volume level is above, say, 20,000 vehicle trips per day. In short, above that level the toll rate would be only one-half cent ($1/2 \cent$) too high or less, and the quantity demanded would be little reduced by such an increase.[w] Below that volume level, discrepancies of up to 10 percent (higher than actual costs) could result and could materially reduce demand. Since the two sets of input data bracket most circumstances, and place the resultant equilibrium flow level between 35,000 and 113,000 daily vehicle trips, it would appear that the calculated volume levels—using linear approximations—are only negligibly low.

Second, the major effect of using linear approximations for the roadway toll functions (in Figure 3-10) is to increase the net revenues (that is, the difference between toll revenues and annual roadway costs), particularly for daily volume levels between 60,000 and 140,000 vehicle trips per day; in this higher volume range, the excess revenues can range between 10 and 30 percent of the necessary roadway costs. For our input data, the daily toll revenues for the high and low demand functions, respectively, were 31 and 6 percent higher than roadway

---

[w]On the other hand, these small increases would produce significant excess profits.

60

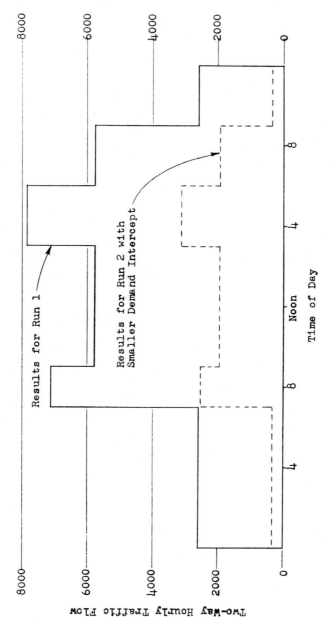

Figure 3–11. Equilibrium Flows Determined by Toll Pricing Linear Program.

costs. Obviously, had it been anticipated that the resultant volume levels would be so high, two or three linear approximations could have been used in place of the single linear function in the volume range between 50,000 and 150,000 daily trips; this would have reduced the excess toll revenue to a fairly low level. (A reduction in the toll would have increased the total volume only slightly, though.)

As a final check of the reasonableness of the model, and its overall predictive characteristics, the hourly volumes during the 4 demand periods were plotted on a time-of-day volume variation chart to provide a visual guide and inspection of the peaking pattern, as shown in Figure 3-11. Both in general and in detail, these daily volume variations bear a "reasonable resemblance" to available empirical evidence. (See Figure 5-3).

In summary, it would appear that utilization of these types of nonlinear models, even when placed within a linear programming format, can provide useful and sufficiently accurate information for the establishment of uniform toll rates and for the determination (or prediction) of resultant travel volumes and congestion. Further, it should be clear that if each of the earlier described price, demand, and roadway toll functions is also subscripted to account for the year-to-year time dimension and especially for the hour-to-hour demand cross-relations (as cited in earlier footnotes) even more realistic long-term results can be obtained.

4

Economic Efficiency, Utilization, Pricing and Investment: The Theoretical Basis

Matters of investment, economic efficiency, utilization, and pricing are significantly related to one another, and involve full knowledge of the cost, price-volume, and demand functions outlined in earlier chapters. The problems of engineering design or planning cannot be extricated from these economic matters, nor can technological developments—as purposeful engineering achievements—be analyzed and evaluated apart from a comprehensive economic analysis dealing with these issues.

This chapter will first include an introductory treatment of investment planning and efficient utilization of facilities and of the alternative means of controlling efficiency and utilization (to include both pricing and other control devices). While the subject will primarily be addressed from the standpoint of economic efficiency, an effort will be made to indicate some of the key implications of cost and benefit incidence. Also, this initial discussion will deal with the benefit and cost consequences stemming from various output, pricing, and expansion situations under conditions of static or constant demand.

Following the development of a general but oversimplified framework pertaining to the static or constant demand conditions, attention will be devoted to the benefit-cost analysis and evaluation procedures required under more realistic conditions of year-to-year and hour-to-hour fluctuations in demand. These procedures will be discussed sequentially for: (1) intertemporal demand fluctuations; (2) intratemporal demand fluctuations; and (3) joint intertemporal and intratemporal demand fluctuations.

The other matter which is given attention in this chapter is that of "backward-bending" or capacity-reducing facilities (that is, situations in which flow increases result in increased delay and in decreased capacity and facility output). Different devices and mechanisms for preventing these capacity-reducing situations are discussed, and their effects on benefits and costs are assessed.

Throughout this chapter's discussion of investment planning, pricing, and efficient utilization measures, *the costs for implementing certain pricing or control devices will NOT be included or considered*; rather, "costless" pricing and control mechanisms will be assumed, thus ignoring any delays or inconveniences to drivers that may result from instituting toll gates or control devices, and neglecting any capital or operating expenditures for the toll collection or control devices. In Chapter 5, this assumption will be relaxed and the consequences or costs of instituting and implementing different sorts of pricing or control devices will be explored.

The three basic assumptions which underlie the entire discussion should be emphasized; (1) goods and services throughout the economy are priced at marginal cost; (2) the commitment of resources to the transport sector will not affect prices for the remainder of the economy or have feedback effects upon the transport demands or upon the costs of providing transport services; and (3) the marginal utility of income is equal for all travelers and is constant over time. In addition, it will be assumed that travelers are homogeneous with respect to their travel time, effort, and money expenditures and that their user "costs" or payments—exclusive of any tolls—are equal to the short-run average variable costs.

It is also important to note that the economic efficiency objective function is presumed to be as follows:

$$\text{Objective} = \text{Maximization of Total Net Benefit};$$

however, this objective function in no way involves the consideration of conflicting or overriding social or political criteria (income redistribution and the like).

4.1 Basic Economic Principles for Providing Transport Services in the Short Run[a]

To begin, the incremental benefit-cost principle is of overriding importance and may be stated as follows: more transport service should be provided so long as the extra or incremental benefit associated with tripmaking is greater than the extra cost incurred for tripmaking; or more simply, one should continue to increase transport output until the marginal benefit is just equal to the marginal cost.[b] In analyzing the incremental benefits, it is necessary to note that the demand function (or, alternatively, the quantity demanded versus "willingness to pay" or price curve) in its inverse form approximates the marginal benefit curve; that is, it describes the increase in total benefit from increasing the hourly flow rate q by one tripmaker.[c] To be more specific, the marginal benefit relationship can be determined as follows for *linear* demand functions of the form:

[a]In this section, and that following, the analysis will be restricted to constant flow situations, both intratemporally and intertemporally. Also, backward-bending cost or price-volume conditions are assumed *not* to exist (see section 4.3).

[b]It is necessary to make the distinction between marginal cost (or benefit) and incremental cost (or benefit), as the terms will be used herein. Marginal cost refers to the increase in total cost which occurs when the transport output or volume is increased by *just one unit*, whereas incremental cost refers to the increase in total cost which occurs when the output or volume is increased *more than one* unit.

[c]Marginal benefit is *not* equivalent to the marginal revenue (or marginal payment) which results from uniform prices; the distinction will be made more precisely later within this section.

$$q = \beta - \alpha p(q) \quad , \tag{4-1}$$

where $p(q)$ is the price which q travelers are willing to pay and α and β are parameters based upon income, population, etc.; then, inverting the demand function shown in equation (4-1), the expression becomes:

$$p(q) = \beta/\alpha - q/\alpha = mb(q) \quad , \tag{4-2}$$

in which the price which q travelers are willing to pay is equal to the marginal benefit or $mb(q)$; i.e., $mb(q)$ is the benefit added by increasing the output q by one more trip.

Also, it should be reemphasized that our primary concern is not focused simply on the incremental *facility* costs which must be incurred to expand or increase output, but on all incremental costs associated with increases in output (to include increments in cost for facilities or vehicles and for private travel time and effort).

Turning first to the short-run situation for a particular facility x, the cost and benefit functions might be as shown in Figure 4-1. In the short-run, the fixed costs[d] will remain the same at high or low levels of output; clearly, in the short-run and over a time period too short to abandon, contract, or expand the facility, they do not affect the level of output if one is concerned with maximizing the total net benefit from use of the facility, without regard for matters of cost and benefit incidence and income distribution. The only costs that are affected by changes in the output level in the short-run are the variable costs; the marginal cost curve or $srmc_x(q)$ measures the unit by unit increase in total variable costs with increases in output. Below output level q_A, and for the cost and demand (or marginal benefit) conditions of Figure 4-1, each successive unit increase in the output level will add more to total benefits than it will add to total costs; that is, $mb(q) > srmc_x(q)$ for $q < q_A$. Thus, total net benefits will continue to increase up to level q_A and at that point or flow level will be equal to:[e]

$$TNB_x(q_A) = \sum_{q=1}^{q_A} mb(q) \; - \; \sum_{q=1}^{q_A} srmc_x(q) \; - \; F_x \quad , \tag{4-3}$$

where $TNB_x(q)$ are the total net benefits (for an hour) for this facility when operated at the output level q. However, for an output above the volume q_A, the

---

[d]Recall that fixed costs are not necessarily the initial costs or capital outlays, but are the opportunity costs of resource inputs which remain constant for levels of output. These costs are not fixed over time, however, since they can be avoided by abandonment or perhaps sale or making another use of the facility; thus, it may be helpful to regard these costs as nonseparable, with respect to output (for a particular facility) in the short-run.

[e]The total net benefits in general, can be positive or negative; at worst, if "efficiently operated," $TNB_x(q) = -F_x$ at $q = 0$. For the illustrative case in Figure 4-1, the total net benefits will be positive (for efficient output).

marginal cost or $srmc_x(q)$ will always exceed the marginal benefit or $mb(q)$, thus decreasing the total net benefit. Also, while each added traveler above q_A but below q_B would *privately* gain from making the trip,[f] the amount *he* would gain would be less than the increment in costs imposed on himself *and* others (which are reflected by the marginal cost or $srmc_x(q)$ curve); thus, the total net benefit would be reduced if the extra q_A to q_B trips were made.

Other aspects are important. If the output level were increased to q_B, the total costs for q_B would still be less than the total benefits for q_B ; the total net benefits or $TNB(q_B)$ would be:

$$TNB(q_B) = \sum_{q=1}^{q_B} mb(q) - VC_x(q_B) - F_x \tag{4-4}$$

$$= \sum_{q=1}^{q_B} mb(q) - \sum_{q=1}^{q_B} srmc_x(q) - F_x \ . \tag{4-5}$$

While for the cost and demand relationships in Figure 4-1, output at q_B would cause no overall loss to society (i.e., total net benefit would be positive), there would be a loss for society relative to the cost and benefit situation for output at

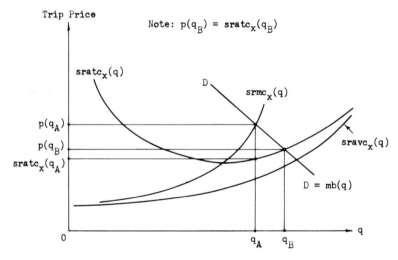

Figure 4-1. Short-Run Cost and Demand Relationships for a Fixed Facility and High Demand (Relative to Cost).

---

[f]That is, each extra traveler between q_A and q_B has an extra benefit of $mb(q)$ which is larger than his *payment of* $sratc_x(q)$, assuming of course that their payments include coverage of both fixed and variable costs (such as travelling on a toll facility).

q_A. In this case, the net loss from increasing output from q_A to q_B or incremental total net benefit $(ITNB_{x,AB})$ will be:

$$ITNB_{x,AB} = TNB_x(q_B) - TNB_x(q_A) \quad , \tag{4-6}$$

and substituting from equations (4-3) and (4-5),

$$ITNB_{x,AB} = \sum_{q=q_A}^{q_B} mb(q) - \sum_{q=q_A}^{q_B} srmc_x(q) \tag{4-7}$$

$$= 1/2(q_B - q_A)\left[p(q_A) + p(q_B)\right]$$

$$+ q_A sravc_x(q_A) - q_B sravc_x(q_B) \quad . \tag{4-8}$$

This expression will result in a negative value.

At this point it is necessary to address the issue of *potential versus actual* benefits and total net benefits. Clearly, if the actual benefits are to be of the magnitude indicated by those which are potential, some device or mechanism must be used to insure that travelers are "segregated" in the fashion indicated by the demand curve. Specifically, to induce the economically efficient results (i.e., those which maximize total net benefit), we must insure that travelers with less than the benefit or trip value at the margin (as defined by their willingness to pay for tripmaking) do not travel in place of others with values which place them above the level at the margin. For example, referring again to Figure 4-1, with the output level which maximized total net benefit (that is, at output q_A), the total net benefit shown by equation (4-3) would be realized only if those travelers with trip values below $p(q_A)$ were excluded and if, therefore, travel were restricted to travelers with equal or higher trip values. Obviously, the price mechanism—at least theoretically—would appear to be the most suitable instrument for effectuating this type of control;[g] in fact, not to use such a device would be to admit, if not guarantee, that the facilities would not actually produce the expected total net benefits. Furthermore, it should be clear that more than the correct (that is, economically efficient) output level—and more than the correct level of capacity and service—is involved here; it is assuring, in addition, that the expected or anticipated benefits do occur.[h] In other words, simple volume controllers (e.g., stop lights, policemen, or electronic controllers)

[g]Until later sections, the problems, costs, and interactions of effective price mechanisms will be ignored; they are hardly trivial or "costless," particularly on the urban scene. However, this is not to suggest that the use of prices does not aid in other important investment planning matters.

[h]This is not to be confused with the compensation principle and related aspects, which are wholly different matters.

could limit the flow using a facility to its "correct" output level, but could (and probably would) result in the actual total net benefits being much lower than the potential total net benefits, because the "wrong" (i.e., lower valued) trips could get there first and preempt the space.

While the price mechanism serves other important purposes in investment planning, it does occupy a central role in assuring that facilities are utilized most efficiently (in economic terms); secondarily (perhaps), its usage impinges on matters of "simple justice" and of insuring that, wherever possible, the costs incurred to provide transport service are paid for by those using and enjoying the benefits of such service. However, an important pricing rule is that only a single uniform price should be charged for the same or identical services, thus disallowing the use of discriminatory pricing (i.e., "charging what the traffic will bear" or charging different prices for the same service according to the value of the service).[i] In brief, this pricing rule is necessary to insure that output is continually increased until the marginal cost and benefit are equal for the last trip, and that transport facilities and services are efficiently utilized.[1]

Once a price mechanism is specified, matters of financial feasibility as well as total net benefit to society (or, say, economic feasibility) can be examined. Again, restricting attention to the short-run conditions characterized in Figure 4-2 (which is a redrafting of those in Figure 4-1, but with the addition of a marginal *revenue* or marginal *payment* curve),[j] we can inquire about alternative prices and their effects on total net benefit and on financial feasibility.

First, different price levels and price policies affect total net benefits to the extent that the quantity demanded, and thus output and benefits, are affected; therefore, the earlier results are still valid. That is, total net benefit will be maximized at an output level equal to q_A when the marginal benefit or price $p(q_A)$ is equal to the short-run marginal cost, or when $p(q_A) = srmc_x(q_A)$.

Second, the total net revenues (or total revenues less total costs)[k] are similarly related to the output level, but bear a different relationship to pricing policy and are maximized under different output and pricing conditions. To

---

[i]Clearly, there are exceptions with respect to discriminatory pricing, some having the full sanction of state and federal regulatory agencies. Governmental agencies permit, if not "force," discriminatory pricing in certain instances to insure that particular services (which are deemed to be "publicly desirable" or "in the public good") continue to be provided even though they may be unprofitable.

[j]Marginal revenue is the increase in total (*not* net) revenue which occurs when the output or volume level is increased by one unit or trip. Also, recognize that in order to increase the output or volume level by one unit the price must be reduced slightly as indicated by the demand curve. Further, the marginal revenue will be positive when the demand is price elastic and negative when the demand is price inelastic. Put differently, price increases will also increase total revenue when the demand is price inelastic, and price decreases will increase total revenue when the demand is price elastic. For a definition of price elasticity and of its relationship to total revenue and marginal revenue, see Appendix 1.

[k]It will be helpful to regard total revenues as total payments by tripmakers, and total net revenues as total net payments (or total payments less total costs). Also, the form of these payments is immaterial, and thus may consist of payments in time, money, or effort, etc.

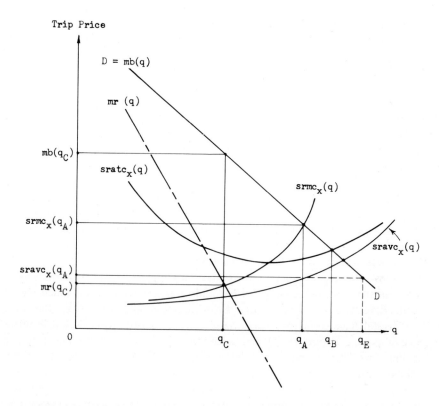

Figure 4-2. Short-Run Cost and Demand Relationships for a Fixed Facility and High Demand (Relative to Cost).

illustrate the relationships, a marginal revenue curve is also shown on Figure 4-2. The marginal revenue curve in this instance indicates the increase in total revenue which will result from increasing the output level one unit, while charging a single uniform price for all trips during a given hour; it must be kept in mind that tripmaking can be increased only by reducing price, and therefore that the extra revenue from an additional tripmaker must be balanced against the reductions in revenue from the previous tripmakers. To calculate total revenues, and in turn the marginal revenues, the demand curve *DD* may be regarded as an average revenue curve (that is, the demand curve expresses the maximum average revenue per traveler to be obtained from *q* travelers—since a uniform price policy is being followed). Thus,

$$TR(q) = q \cdot p(q) \quad , \tag{4-9}$$

where $TR(q)$ is the total revenue from q travelers. The marginal revenue or $mr(q)$ is simply the differential of the total revenue function with respect to flow, or:[1]

$$mr(q) \doteq \frac{dTR(q)}{dq} \quad ; \tag{4-10}$$

using the inverse form of the linear demand function, as shown in equation (4-2), substituting into equation (4-9), and then differentiating,

$$mr(q) = \beta/\alpha - 2q/\alpha \quad ; \tag{4-11}$$

this linear marginal revenue function is shown in Figure 4-2.

Faced with these short-run supply and demand conditions, and with a uniform (single) price, it should be evident that each increase in output up to level q_C will increase total net revenues (since the marginal revenue is greater than marginal cost up to that point); output above or below that point will not maximize total net revenues. However, it is also apparent that a uniform (single) price equal to $mr(q_C) = srmc_x(q_C)$ would clear the market at a much higher output level. Accordingly, in order to maximize total net revenues, the price level would have to be set at $p(q_C)$ and "excess" profits would result.[m] While such a pricing policy would maximize financial returns in the short-run, it certainly would not maximize total net benefits (from the standpoint of the general public).

Furthermore, while this type of pricing policy could only be exercised under monopoly conditions, it should be noted that governmental agencies responsible for the construction, operation, control, and pricing of highway facilities often do find themselves somewhat in this monopoly position and could (and sometimes do) take advantage of such stringent revenue producing policies. On the other hand, were the objective function of maximizing total net benefits to be followed by governmental agencies, the pricing policy to be adopted would be that to insure that the output level were q_A. In this instance, the price would be set equal to $srmc_x(q)$ covering short-run marginal costs and clearing the market.[n] However, even when following this marginal cost pricing policy and for

---

[1] As before, the differential is simply an approximation for $\dfrac{\Delta TR(q)}{\Delta q}$.

[m] By "excess" profits, it is meant that profits (net of total costs) over and above the normal return on invested capital (or opportunity costs) will be accrued; $sratc_x(q_C)$ includes an allowance for normal return.

[n] The expression "clearing the market" means that all persons desiring to travel at the quoted price will be able to make the trip; thus, with the price set at $p(q_A) = srmc_x(q_A)$, all travelers with a trip value of equal or higher value will be able to travel (since the output level is q_A). On the other hand, if the output were restricted to q_A and if the price were set at $sravc_x(q_A)$, the market for tripmaking (or number who desired to travel at that price) would be much higher than the available "supply" (i.e., q_E would desire to travel) and the market would not be cleared.

the specific demand conditions illustrated in Figure 4-2, it can be seen that "excess" profits will accrue; that is, the total revenues will be greater than total costs (with normal return on capital included) and total net revenues will be greater than zero.

What happens to these excess profits? Do they affect the short-run pricing policy? From the standpoint of economic efficiency (and assuming a total lack of concern for who pays and who benefits and for matters of income-redistribution) *in the short run*, the correct pricing policy is clearcut—short-run marginal cost pricing.[o] However, *in the long-run*, while such a policy is also consistent (at least for the basic underlying assumptions reiterated in the introduction to this chapter), there is obvious appeal for considering the expansion possibilities.

In summary, should governmental agencies adopt a long-run view with respect to system or facility expansion, and in the absence of any concern for distributional questions, the pricing policy is reasonably clearcut, at least for conditions assumed throughout and for the cost and demand conditions shown in Figure 4-2.[2] Finally, for this first case, it can be seen from Figure 4-2, and from our earlier assumption, that the perceived payments by travelers (exclusive of any tolls) were equal to the short-run average variable costs, that the necessary toll charge required to bring the total perceived payments per trip up to the short-run marginal cost (at the level of maximum economic efficiency) would be equal to $srmc_x(q_A)$ minus $sravc_x(q_A)$.

A more ambiguous short-run situation is depicted in Figure 4-3. As before, the best output level from the standpoint of maximizing total net benefit, would be that corresponding to an equality between marginal benefits (as represented by the demand curve $D'D'$) and short-run marginal costs, or would be an output equal to q_G. Since the fixed costs cannot be altered *in the short run*, they do not affect decisions in the short-run regarding proper level or output. At the same time, though, it should be evident that private firms could not long endure a short-run marginal cost pricing solution in cost and demand situations of this sort; that is, from the standpoint of *financial* feasibility, marginal cost pricing (with uniform single prices) would produce total revenues that run less than the total costs (including normal return on capital). Specifically, the total net revenue loss at an output level of q_G and price equal to $p(q_G) = srmc_x(q_G)$ would be:

$$TNR(q_G) = q_G \left[srmc_x(q_G) - sratc_x(q_G) \right] . \qquad (4\text{-}12)$$

Of course, if either government agencies or private firms held a monopoly position (the former often do), and desired to maximize total net revenue, then output would be adjusted to level q_J by charging a price of $p(q_J)$; in this instance, while total net benefit would not be maximized (in the short-run), financial security would be assured as total revenues would exceed the short-run

---

[o]Again, ignoring the difficulties and costs of implementing such a policy.

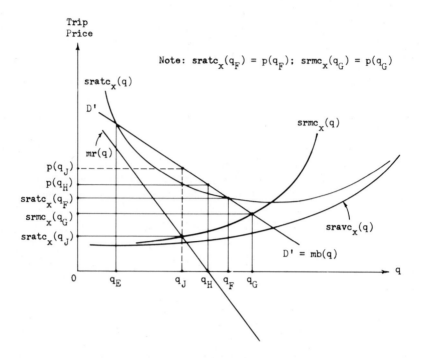

Figure 4-3. Short-Run Cost and Demand Relationships for a Fixed Facility and Low Demand (Relative to Cost).

total costs (with normal return on capital included). Alternatively, financial security could be maintained by adopting average cost pricing and adjusting output to level q_F, by charging a price of $p(q_F) = sratc_x(q_F)$. While it is obvious that in either of these cases total net benefits would not be maximized, and that the economy would suffer (to the extent of the loss or decrease in total net benefits, relative to the maximum which could be obtained), no subsidy would be required and no threat of financial infeasibility would result.

Four aspects arise and should be considered.[3] One, is this short-run picture (shown in Figure 4-3) typical of the long-run expectations? Two, should one consider the use of subsidies to make up the difference between total costs and total revenues which would occur at an output of q_G and with a price of $p(q_G)$? Three, should some sort of discriminatory pricing or perhaps a multipart tariff be employed, such that revenues and costs are balanced? Four, can important inconsistencies develop between the private and public sectors of the economy?

If over the long-run, the demand and cost conditions are such that the short-run and temporary financially infeasible conditions will be overcome, then short-run marginal cost pricing should be pursued for maximum economic efficiency and no conflict will exist between economic efficiency and financial security. However, assuming this is not the case, the other aspects are open for consideration. From the standpoint of economic efficiency, the "correct" solution is to price at marginal cost and subsidize the facility or venture, *whether it be a public or private project*. Thus, one might be led to conclude that subsidization of the losses is preferable and warranted (aside from distributional matters). However, such a position is much too naive, and overlooks the inconsistencies with respect to private and public sectors that do exist and that doubtlessly will continue to exist.

As a practical matter, private industry in analyzing and evaluating alternative projects does not, upon finding itself in a decreasing returns to scale situation (such as shown in Figure 4-3), usually or even often undertake the program because the overall net benefits of the economy are enhanced, nor does it usually try to obtain the necessary subsidy from local, state, or federal sources. As a consequence, to consistently subsidize public programs *on just this basis* (and aside from other social or political criteria) would in all likelihood bring about double standards with regard to investment planning and produce unknown consequences with respect to overall economic efficiency. Also, and in contrast to the situation for externalities, it seems reasonable to argue (somewhat heuristically) that a policy which endorsed the subsidy of all public and only some private programs having increasing returns to scale would virtually assure overinvestment in the public sector and probably would result in less than optimum allocation of resources. In short, while the public projects adopted through subsidization would demonstrate overall economic feasibility (i.e., positive total net benefits), it seems likely that on occasion private use of the resources—with subsidy, if necessary—would produce higher total net benefits. These qualifications make it difficult to reach any general conclusions regarding the worthwhileness of always subsidizing public projects having increasing returns to scale, and emphasize the necessity of a more comprehensive analysis than can be undertaken herein.

Two other "solutions" to be used for overcoming financial infeasibility in falling cost situations (such as that shown in Figure 4-3) are discriminatory prices or multipart tariffs. While a variety of these practices can be, and often are, used successfully to eliminate financial deficits, it should be recognized that their usage forces abandonment of the "equal price to all rule" and, as a consequence, makes it impossible to conclude in general that the resultant project will or will not produce optimal efficiency.[4]

4.2 Basic Economic Principles for the Long-Run

The principles outlined in the previous section apply with equal force for long-run situations, though with some important conditions and additions. Let us examine two cases, the first regarding situations characterized by constant returns to scale,[p] and the second for those with other than constant returns to scale; both will be examined while assuming that demand functions do not vary from time interval to time interval or from time period to time period (i.e., demand does not vary intratemporally or intertemporally).

The constant-returns case is illustrated in Figure 4-4, in addition to the short-run cost relationships for two possible facilities, y and z. For this long-run situation, the long-run marginal cost curve serves to measure the extra costs (whether fixed or variable) associated with successive unit increases in output as facility size is altered; as before, the demand curve is the marginal benefit function. Since the marginal benefit is greater than long-run marginal cost up to output level q_C, total net benefit will continue to increase for expansion up to that flow level; at that point total net benefit is maximized, thus indicating the long-run optimum output level and the optimum-sized facility. A price equal to the long-run marginal cost, or $p(q_C) = lrmc(q_C) = srmc_z(q_C)$, will clear the market and insure a quantity demanded consistent with the optimum output level; facility z would be the optimum. Furthermore, it can be seen that for this special case the price is equal to the long-run average cost, thus assuring financial feasibility and resulting in no ambiguities. The total revenues will just equal the total costs, and the total net benefits will be equal to the following:

$$TNB(q_C) = \sum_{q=1}^{q_C} mb(q) - \sum_{q=1}^{q_C} lrmc(q) \qquad (4\text{-}13)$$

$$= \sum_{q=1}^{q_C} mb(q) - LRTC(q_C) \quad . \qquad (4\text{-}14)$$

Under competitive conditions, both private and public incentives will be sufficient to bring about expansion to the appropriate facility and output level; both public and private objectives (maximum total net benefits for the former and maximum total net revenues for the latter) will result in the same solution, thus offering no conflict. Finally, if we again assume that travelers perceive the travel costs (aside from any tolls) according to the short-run average variable costs (for whatever facility is in existence), then it is evident that a toll equal to $lrmc(q_C)$ minus $sravc_z(q_C)$ will be required in order to insure that the quantity demanded is consistent with the optimum output level, and that the actual benefits are consistent with those necessary to produce the most efficient solution. (In other words, if volume controllers instead of prices were used as a mechanism for insuring the proper output, then travelers with trip values or marginal travel benefits less than marginal costs associated with their tripmaking

[p]Recall that, for constant returns to scale situations, percentage increases in output result in equal percentage increases in total cost, for all levels of output; thus the long-run average total cost remains constant and is equal to the long-run marginal cost.

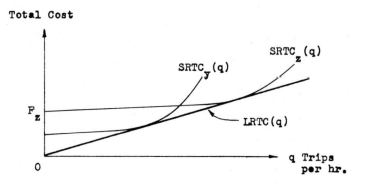

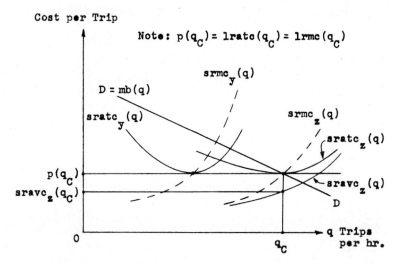

Figure 4–4. Long-Run Demand and Cost Relationships for Constant Returns to Scale.

could preempt the space, causing total benefits and net benefits to be decreased.^{q}

Furthermore, it can be seen that for this long-run, constant-returns situation the necessary toll (for most efficient utilization) will be equal to the unit fixed cost for the optimum sized facility.^{r} That is, assuming that facility z is the optimum facility size, the following relationship would hold:

$$F_z = (q_C)\left[srmc_x(q_C) - sravc_z(q_C)\right] \tag{4-15}$$

$$= (q_C)(TOLL) \quad , \tag{4-16}$$

or

$$TOLL = F_z/q_C \quad . \tag{4-17}$$

The costs for other than constant returns to scale are shown in Figure 4-5; for an output level below q_{min} there are increasing returns to scale (i.e., economies of scale), and above that level there are decreasing returns to scale (i.e., diseconomies of scale).^{s} In addition to the long-run marginal and average cost functions, the short-run cost curves are shown for just two of the possible facilities, A and C. Also, two different demand conditions, DD and $D'D'$, are illustrated.

Notice, first, that in this illustration it is assumed that some minimum level of nonseparable costs or F must be incurred before even one unit of output can be provided, and that these costs do not vary with output;^{t} implied is some degree of indivisibility or that, for example, a minimum amount of right-of-way and at least one lane of roadway or one track of railroad must be provided before any movement can take place. While these costs are fixed with respect to the output level (i.e., they do not vary with output) and are common to the total amount of tripmaking which will occur, over the long-run they can, of course, be avoided. (Recall that these are the opportunity costs, and where they apply to an existing facility, they are not equivalent to the original capital outlays—or opportunity

---

^{q}More specifically, by using volume instead of price controllers, travelers having trip values falling between $p(q_C)$ and $sravc_C(q_C)$—the latter of which is lower—could preempt some of the roadway space in place of travelers having trip values of $p(q_C)$ or higher.

^{r}The assumption is made as before about perceived user payments being equal to short-run average variable costs.

^{s}If you like, the first case can be termed that of "falling average cost" and the second that of "rising average cost."

^{t}Clearly, these costs (or F) are not fixed with respect to time—as the entire facility and service can be abandoned, thus avoiding these costs. Hereafter, these nonseparable costs may be termed "threshold costs."

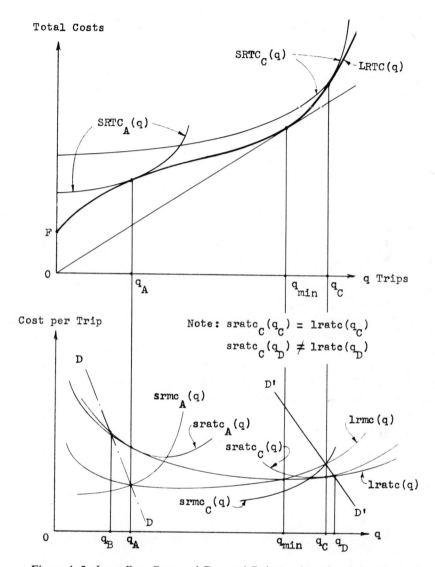

Figure 4–5. Long-Run Cost and Demand Relationships for Other than Constant Returns to Scale.

costs of resources foregone at the time of construction[u]—but they are equal to the current alternative opportunity costs. As a consequence, not to abandon the facility entirely would be to forfeit these alternative opportunities, and thus to incur these "foregone opportunity" costs.)

Since the threshold costs or F vary over the long-run (that is, they can be avoided over the long-run), they must be considered in matters of economic efficiency, as well as in those involving financial feasibility. As we shall see, the threshold costs are not directly involved in a determination of the proper price, but only in ascertaining the overall or aggregate economic and financial feasibility.

More simply, over the long-run, both the marginal costs *and* threshold costs must be exceeded by the total benefits accruing from usage if the investment is to be regarded as economically feasible from a public point of view.

The necessary relationships between costs and benefits are as follows (for the optimum facility and for most efficient usage of it):[v]

$$LRTC(q_o) = \sum_{q=1}^{q_o} lrmc(q) + F \quad , \tag{4-18}$$

in which

$$lrmc(q) \doteq \frac{dLRTC(q)}{dq} \quad , \tag{4-19}$$

and q_o is the optimum output level. For long-run economic efficiency and feasibility, the following condition must also hold (in addition to marginal benefit = long-run marginal cost):

$$\sum_{q=1}^{q_o} mb(q) \geqslant \sum_{q=1}^{q_o} lrmc(q) + F \tag{4-20}$$

$$\geqslant LRTC(q_o) \quad . \tag{4-21}$$

As before, it can be concluded that the *most* economically efficient (nonzero),[w] though not necessarily feasible, level of output will be that at which the marginal benefit (as defined by the demand curve) is just equal to the

---

[u]The original outlays are "sunk" and irrecoverable; at this stage, the only thing that matters is what other uses can be made of the facility land and structures.

[v]Ignore, for the time being, problems of discounting costs and benefits occurring during different years; this will be covered in a later section.

[w]The use of the word "nonzero" is crucial, as will be explained in succeeding paragraphs; also, it is important to note that this full statement, with no further qualification, applies to well-behaved functions. (Otherwise, multiple equalities and ambiguous answers can occur.)

long-run marginal cost. Turning first to the low demand (or increasing returns) case, which occurs with the demand function DD in Figure 4-5, one would conclude that the *most* efficient *nonzero* output level would be q_A and that the proper facility would be A. This follows, since each increase in output up to level q_A has marginal benefits which are greater than the long-run marginal costs; this holds true even when losses occur at low output levels, since any losses sustained for low output levels would be continually decreased up to output q_A.[x] The next key question (from an overall economic efficiency standpoint) is therefore: Do the marginal benefits *in total* (at optimum nonzero output) exceed the long-run costs in total? In this case, that shown in Figure 4-5 with demand curve DD, it is clear that the total benefits *do* exceed the long-run costs in total, since at output level q_B the demand curve intersects the long-run average cost curve.[y] However, had the demand curve fallen below the long-run average cost curve at all output levels, then without summing the benefits and costs, it would not be possible to tell whether the total net benefits were positive or negative.

As for matters of pricing and financial feasibility, the problem is little different from that outlined for the short-run case. With a single uniform price, and with marginal cost pricing, the best price for this situation—from the standpoint of economic efficiency to the overall economy—would be $p(q_A) = lrmc(q_A) = srmc(q_A)$; this price clearly falls below the long-run average total cost of $lratc(q_A)$ and will result in a total *financial* deficit of q_A times the difference between $lratc(q_A)$ and $lrmc(q_A)$. The problem is as before: Should the project be subsidized? Should multipart prices be used to make up deficits? And, as before, one might conclude (in the absence of more comprehensive analyses) that unless all private and public projects falling into this category are subsidized to the extent of the deficits, no public project should be subsidized on these grounds (again, aside from other criteria and distributional matters).

One difficulty with this "simple-minded" view, of course, is that competitive private industries faced with this particular increasing returns to scale and demand situation would find the project feasible even when using uniform prices; that is, they would undertake the project and produce only up to output level q_B, while pricing the service at $lratc(q_B)$. In the process, society would forfeit the gains from increasing output still further; thus arises the plea for multipart prices or some form of price discrimination.[z] Also, since industry

---

[x]This assumes the existence of "well-behaved" cost functions.

[y]In other words, for output level q_B, we know that total benefits exceed total costs (by an amount equal to the total consumer surpluses for q_B, given average cost pricing), and from output level q_B to q_A, the total net benefits increase still further, since the marginal benefits exceed the long-run marginal costs for each output point inbetween.

[z]The private firm would also prefer to produce at the higher output level, since profits would be increased still further—*assuming* of course that some form of price discrimination can be used to cover the deficits which would result from uniform pricing. Further, one can argue that private firms, in many instances, use product differentiation and "subtle" markups for products in the higher quality portion of the range as a means of price discrimination and a way of covering deficits which would occur with a uniform price (at marginal cost) for each different product.

certainly *will* undertake the project (and gain normal profits from so doing and producing at level q_B), two obvious questions arise: (1) Why don't governments *always* subsidize such situations? (2) Should not public investments of the same sort (i.e., increasing returns and sufficiently high demand to insure that total benefits exceed total costs) always be undertaken? As for the first question, some would argue that most of the projects or situations of this sort either fall within the public sector or (ultimately, at least) are taken over by the government, thus *permitting* them to be consistently subsidized. However, it is difficult to argue the validity of this view;[aa] further, it is difficult to argue that government policy follows a consistent and "proper" marginal cost pricing policy. As for the second question, and when faced with the fact that private industry will undertake projects of this sort (and that they seldom will price at marginal cost and be subsidized to the extent of the long-run losses), it is difficult to gauge whether for similar situations the adoption of public invest- ments and use of marginal cost pricing will enhance economic efficiency. We are confronted with second-best considerations and can reach no general conclu- sions, other than to say that it is obvious that "double standards" are used in the private and public sectors.

The second case shown in Figure 4-5, that of decreasing returns to scale (i.e., rising average costs) when the demand function is $D'D'$, represents no conflict to either private industry or the economy at large.[bb] Faced with this situation, either private or public transport agencies would (under perfect competition) continue to expand capacity to that of facility C and service up to output level q_C. The price necessary to maximize total net benefits and to clear the market at this output level would be $p(q_C) = lrmc(q_C)$, a price level which is higher of course than $lratc(q_C)$ and the short-run average total cost as well.[cc] Since the unit price is greater than the long-run average total cost (which includes an allowance for normal profits on capital), "excess" profits and revenues to the extent of the difference will accrue (to someone). But these excess profits would hardly induce expansion beyond this point for economic efficiency or financial reasons, either in the short-run or long-run; in both instances, for higher output, both the marginal and incremental costs would exceed the marginal and incremental benefits and revenues, reducing total net benefits to society and total net revenues, and indicating that neither public agencies nor "benevolent" private firms would expand further. From a net revenue standpoint (and with a single uniform price), a similar result obtains: in order to increase the quantity demanded the price would have to be lowered, placing it below both short-run and long-run marginal costs and therefore producing losses (relative to output at q_C). Thus, profit motives would hardly induce entry into the market by other

---

[aa]The automotive industry and many privately-financed toll road projects are but two examples of situations in which the arguments fail.

[bb]Ruling out monopoly situations, and the like.

[cc]$lratc(q_C) = sratc(q_C)$.

producers, or expansion by either private or public agencies (that is, for other than distributional or other equity matters).

The conclusions in this section can be summarized by stating the necessary conditions for economic efficiency and feasibility; however, the third condition stated below only applies in those instances when all economically feasible projects or planning programs *must also* be financially feasible (and can cause less than the most economically efficient capacity and output level to be adopted). The conditions are:

(a) Total benefits must equal or exceed total costs:[dd]

$$\sum_{q=1}^{q_o} mb(q) \geqslant \sum_{q=1}^{q_o} lrmc(q) + F \quad . \tag{4-22}$$

(b) Efficient utilization and equilibrium flow:

$$Price \ = \ lrmc(q_o) \ = \ srmc_o(q_o) \tag{4-23}$$

$$= \ mb(q_o) \quad . \tag{4-24}$$

(c) No subsidy:[ee]

$$Price \ \geqslant \ lratc(q_o) \quad . \tag{4-25}$$

4.3 The "Bottleneck" or Backward-Bending Case[5]

Various transport facilities have design or control characteristics that permit backward-bending or capacity-reducing situations to develop;[ff] that is, once the entering or input traffic volumes reach or approach some critical level, intervehicle behavior is such that shock waves and stop-and-go traffic flow result. This intervehicle behavior often reduces the effective traffic-carrying capacity of,

---

[dd]Only uniform single prices are considered; let facility o be regarded as the optimum sized facility and let q_o be the optimum output.

[ee]This restriction might be applied, unless *all* public and private projects having decreasing returns to scale and sufficiently high demand—and meeting the other necessary conditions—are subsidized, though not for reasons of economic efficiency.

[ff]For these purposes, it is not necessary to define precisely what types of facilities and flow conditions exhibit these characteristics. However, as a general guide, it can be noted that uncontrolled expressways and throughways (or those having no controls on input) often have backward-bending or capacity reducing conditions, while facilities having entry controls of some sort, such as signalized or police controlled intersections, do not have backward-bending characteristics. In the first case, both capacity (or volume carrying capability) and travel delay is dependent on the arrival rates or entering flow, while in the latter, capacity (but not travel delay) is independent of the arrival rate.

and increases delay on, the roadways. Capacity reduction can continue so long as the input rate is sustained at, or above, some critical level. While intervehicle flow dynamics are not yet sufficiently well understood, the above remarks and the general diagram in Figure 4-6 probably characterize the phenomenon appropriately. Referring to Figure 4-6, the dashed-line portion of the curve illustrates flow and capacity-reduction behavior for capacity-reducing types of facilities, once input volumes approach or exceed the maximum or capacity flow rate V_m and cause shock-wave action; the solid-line portion of the curve above point m represents flow behavior for non-capacity-reducing types of facilities.[gg]

At the outset, it is evident that economies could be effected (i.e., efficiency could be improved) by the use of devices of one sort or another to limit entry and thus prevent shock-wave action and avoid capacity-reducing situations; the objective would simply be to prevent the input volume rate from approaching "too closely" the capacity volume rate at the bottleneck section. One simple device for insuring that the input volume rate is properly controlled would be to install input volume entry controllers (such as stop lights) on ramps, in order to

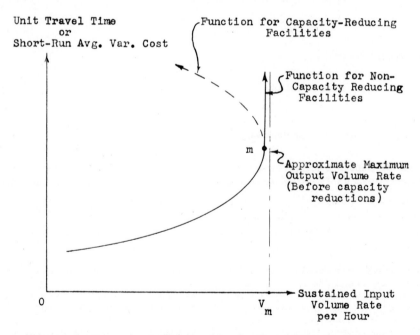

Figure 4-6. Approximate Relationships for Travel Time (or Cost) Versus Flow for Capacity-Reducing and Noncapacity Reducing Facilities.

[gg]Facilities *without* input-output controls (or uncontrolled facilities) will be described as "backward-bending" or capacity-reducing types, and those with input-output controls, as non-capacity-reducing types.

insure that the entering volume was reasonably uniform and did not exceed (or approach too closely) output capacity. Another device which could be used is tolls, as is sometimes suggested by economists.

In considering the use of tolls to control backward-bending situations, three cases would appear possible and worthy of consideration:[hh] two of these are shown in Figures 4-7 and 4-8. In Case 1, that shown in Figure 4-7, where the demand curve *DD* intersects with the "cost"-volume curve[ii] *below* the maximum flow point, capacity reduction situations will not arise (other than momentarily) even under existing average variable cost pricing, since the quantity demanded will not be high enough to approach the critical or maximum flow rate, and thus produce shock-wave action and capacity reductions; also, it should be noted that the intersection of the demand curve with the "cost"–volume curve, at point *a* on the backward-bending portion of the latter curve, is (in most cases) a "fiction." Quite simply, the roadway usage could never stabilize at this point, since a *sustained* input volume rate at that low level *(V$_a$)* would be below the critical or maximum flow-rate point, and thus the shock-wave action would quickly subside and congestion would cease. However, it should be noted that in this case (where the quantity demanded is below the maximum flow rate point)

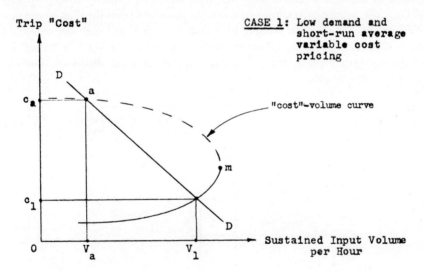

Figure 4-7. Short-Run Variable Cost and Demand Conditions for Backward-Bending Situations: Case 1.

[hh]Note, however, that the discussion ignores the extra costs and delays stemming from installation and operation of such controllers, a matter that is not insignificant.

[ii]Again, this is the short-run average variable cost curve; unless specified differently, any future use of the term "cost"–volume curve (or trip "cost") can be interpreted similarly.

fairly temporary and short shock-wave action and backward-bending situations can occur if the input volume rate fluctuates sufficiently to produce monetary, *as opposed to sustained*, rates that approach or exceed the critical maximum flow level. Finally, then, for case 1, all of the remarks in the previous two sections on pricing apply directly to this situation, with no modification.

Case 2 (as shown in Figure 4-8) illustrates the situation where demand is sufficiently high to cause backward-bending and capacity-reducing situations to develop when short-run average variable cost pricing is in force; in such cases it should be clear that capacity reductions work to the detriment of all. Consequently, if by some manner the input volume rate can be prevented from exceeding (or approaching too closely) the critical or maximum output flow rate (V_m), capacity reductions will not take place, and less congestion will result for the same (or even a higher) volume. Referring to the "cost" and demand curves of Case 2 in Figure 4-8, under short-run average variable cost pricing, one might be led to believe that equilibrium would be established at point b with volume V_1 and "cost" (or "price" to the traveler) c_1. As mentioned before, this situation probably cannot develop more than momentarily, since a *sustained* input-volume of V_1 would cause the travel "cost" to fall to the level c_1'; in turn, this lower "cost" (c_1') would tend to cause the volume to increase far above the critical or maximum output flow rate, thus producing capacity reductions and limiting the quantity demanded. It can be hypothesized that the flow would not stabilize, but would keep shifting back and forth between high and low flow rates. Even so, the apparent or "fictitious" equilibrium point b is useful for estimating suitable tolls for preventing capacity-reducing situations. For ex-

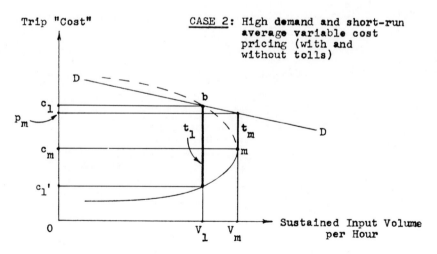

Figure 4–8. Short-Run Variable Cost and Demand Conditions for Backward-Bending Situations: Case 2.

ample, with a toll of t_1 (equal to c_1 minus c_1'), capacity reductions would not result; and further, it would appear that both volume and total unit cost *to the traveler* (variable "cost" plus toll) would be maintained (other than for temporary fluctuations) at roughly the same low volume and high cost positions that occurred without tolls, but with the added toll (t_1) just offsetting the time delay cost which was avoided (or c_1 minus c_1').[jj] Perhaps a "better" solution to this situation would be to impose a toll of t_m (or one just slightly larger), which would then lead to equilibrium at roughly the maximum flow V_m, and to a lowering of total unit costs to travelers, the latter to include both variable "costs" and tolls. (Some liberty is being taken in suggesting that equilibrium could be established at, or almost exactly at, the maximum flow point; however, this impropriety will be overlooked.)

Between the two toll possibilities just suggested, which is better? And from what point of view? Also, are there other price or control mechanisms which are more suitable?

Certainly, as far as the travelers are concerned, a toll of t_m is preferable (overall) to one of t_1 or to no toll (and no control).[kk] A toll of t_m would result in the *users'* total net benefits being increased by an amount of $1/2(V_1 + V_m)(c_1 - p_m)$ over those which they would accrue with either no tolls or a toll of t_1; this gain to travelers would result even aside from additional benefits they might accrue from distribution of the toll revenue pool (which is equal to $V_m t_m$). However, the travelers *could* gain even more in total net benefit increases, should physical volume controllers (such as signals) be used instead of tolls to limit flow to V_m, *and* should the same people as would travel with a toll of t_m continue to travel, the latter possibility being highly unlikely, however. But were this unlikely circumstance to occur, the travelers' gain in total net benefit (relative to no tolls or to a toll of t_1) *could* be equal to $1/2(V_1 + V_m)(c_1 - p_m)$ plus $V_m t_m$.

Next, of course, it is appropriate to consider the costs and benefits from a broader point of view (i.e., in terms of overall economic efficiency); for this purpose, and to simplify the exposition, let us assume that *all* "fixed" or nonseparable costs are sunk and thus that only variable costs are of concern.[ll] The average variable (or average total) cost curve for flow levels below the critical level, or for flow levels below the point where backward-bending

---

[jj]While this conclusion is "suggested," it cannot be stated firmly because of the dynamic, traffic fluctuating situation which would exist without tolls and which distorts any equilibrium situations. Also, it might be helpful to note that uniform tolls of this sort would, *in effect* (but not actually), simply decrease the demand function intercept by that amount.

[kk]It is of some importance to note that consideration is restricted to average variable costs and tolls, and to just one economic group (i.e., the costs and benefits are not assessed without regard for distributional matters, etc.).

[ll]Under these circumstances, the short-run average variable and average total costs are identical.

situations are created, would be that indicated by the solid-line curve below point m on Figure 4-9; also, if the flow were controlled (e.g., by flow controllers and/or tolls), such that shock-waves and backward-bending cost situations could not occur, the average variable cost curve for *higher* levels of *input* flow (that is, for input volumes greater than V_m) would be that of the solid line portion above point m. Here, of course, it is necessary to make a distinction between input and output, and to note that input volumes greater than V_m would imply that queues, delays, and costs would be increasing indefinitely, or as long as flows were sustained above V_m, and until the queue was worked off. Thus, while a volume of V_m would be the constant *output*, the cost would be indefinitely high, at least so long as the input volume was sustained at levels greater than V_m and a queue remained.

The marginal cost curve shown on Figure 4-9 would apply only to the circumstances for controlled flow conditions and for the solid line portion of the average variable cost curve.

For the circumstances depicted in Figure 4-9, under marginal cost pricing an equilibrium flow of V_h and a price of p_e (to include a toll equal to p_e minus c_h) would result and the total net benefits would be:

$$TNB(V_h) = \sum_{q=1}^{V_h} mb(q) - \sum_{q=1}^{V_h} srmc(q) \qquad (4\text{-}26)$$

Note: b and f are fictional equilibrium points.
$$c_h = sravc(V_h)$$

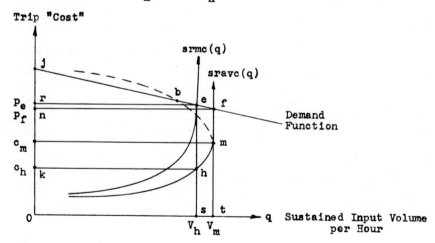

Figure 4–9. Short-Run Cost and Demand Conditions for Backward-Bending Situations.

$$= \sum_{q=1}^{V_h} mb(q) - (V_h) \left[sravc(V_h) \right] \quad . \tag{4-27}$$

The total net benefits for marginal cost pricing, shown in equation (4-27), can be shown to be equal to area *jkhe* (or, area *jose* minus *kosh*).

Since for flows greater than V_h the marginal costs are greater than the marginal benefits (the latter as measured by the demand function), any solution to increase the flow beyond V_h can only reduce the total net benefits and reduce economic efficiency, even if tolls are combined with volume controllers. As a consequence, the earlier solution—of average variable cost pricing plus a toll of t_m—which maximized the total net benefits *for travelers* would not represent the pricing policy of highest overall economic efficiency, and a loss to society would result from the use of a toll equal to t_m. The extent of the loss in economic efficiency would be as follows:

Economic Efficiency *Loss* Stemming from Use of a Toll Equal to t_m

$$= \sum_{q=V_h}^{V_m} mb(q) - \sum_{q=V_h}^{V_m} srmc(q) \tag{4-28}$$

$$= 1/2(V_m - V_h)(p_e + p_f)$$

$$-(V_m c_m - V_h c_h) \quad . \tag{4-29}$$

In summary, because of the relationship between marginal costs and marginal benefits for flow levels between V_h and V_m, we can conclude that $TNB(V_h) > TNB(V_m)$ and that marginal cost pricing will lead to the most economically efficient solution even in backward-bending situations. (A similar line of reasoning can be applied to the long-run pricing and expansion situation as well.)

4.4 Efficiency and Investment As Related to Demand Fluctuations

By and large, the remarks in earlier sections characterized static travel situations and ignored the complexities which are introduced by considering the highly dynamic nature of investment and demand. While in the former cases, deterministic approaches to establishment of the "optimum" size facility and output level appeared to be possible, in a dynamic and more practical setting such an opportunity appears increasingly difficult, unfeasible, and perhaps impossible.

Moreover, it seems fair to say that many of the difficulties arising from a more comprehensive treatment of the dynamic conditions stem from the rigidity of engineering practice. To be more specific, highway transport engineers (in particular) commonly adopt design standards which, as a practical matter, introduce self-imposed and artificial technological and cost indivisibilities;[mm] these indivisibilities in turn do not permit year-to-year tailoring of technology to the year-by-year cost and benefit circumstances, and they inevitably lead to situations of severe overcapacity or undercapacity with their concomitant economic consequences. And, these rigidities and artificial indivisibilities make it increasingly costly to take advantage of technological progress.

The combination of these difficulties makes it necessary to place the investment planning problem within the more usual type of benefit-cost analysis framework, in which particular facility designs, staging plans, and pricing policies are analyzed and evaluated with respect to their costs and benefits (or revenues, where necessary). The most suitable type of benefit-cost analysis and evaluation procedure, and that which will be followed throughout the remainder of this book, is termed the present worth, present value, or net present value method, the latter term being more preferable;[nn] such a procedure, while less common *to the engineer* than the benefit-cost ratio, internal rate-of-return, or equivalent annual cost methods, avoids a number of practical and technical difficulties and inconsistencies which often arise with use of the last three methods. Because of the wide coverage of the general subject area of benefit-cost analysis procedures, no attempt will be made to explain or detail the reasons for adopting the net present value method in preference to the other procedures.[6]

In this section, the benefit-cost analysis procedures will be applied to design situations involving three different types of demand fluctuations: first, with respect to intertemporal (or year-to-year) demand fluctuations, while assuming there are no intratemporal (or hour-to-hour) demand fluctuations; second, with respect to intratemporal demand fluctuations, while assuming there are no intertemporal changes; and third, with respect to both (that is, joint) intratemporal and intertemporal changes.

4.4.1 Intertemporal Demand Fluctuations and Efficiency[oo]

First, recognize that the essential problem is to determine how much of an investment to make and how large a facility to build (or to which level we should expand) *now*, in light of expectations about present and future costs, demands, and benefits. A planning horizon is clearly implied, and also a staging

---

[mm]Admittedly, railroad and air transport facilities and systems are less divisible (and thus less subject to this problem) than highway transport facilities, but not so much as one might suspect at first glance.

[nn]The terms "net present value" and "total discounted net benefit" will be used interchangeably throughout.

[oo]The remarks in this section apply only to situations in which there are no intratemporal or hour-to-hour demand fluctuations.

plan within those time limits. Required is knowledge of year-to-year demand expectations, year-to-year cost functions *for each staging plan*, and year-to-year discount rates, all properly accounting for the uncertainties of man and nature, and for differences between market and opportunity values. Further, there are problems involving the extra delays, interruptions, and other such costs occurring during construction and maintenance periods, and there are the practical considerations involving workable pricing mechanisms, steady versus fluctuating prices, and so forth.

While it is necessary to anticipate and account for the entire stream of expected future costs and benefits in the process of making decisions about *today's* commitments, once a decision is made about present actions, there is clearly no firm commitment being made with respect to future ones. One commitment does not *require* the other, after the fact; on the other hand, the earlier action can and probably will affect later actions, even in the face of changes in expected benefits or costs, if for no other reason, because earlier commitments (usually) can be regarded as sunk.

Another important aspect, based upon the analyses and conclusions earlier in this chapter, is that it is not necessary to place fixed and variable costs on commensurate scales with respect to *specific* time intervals and output levels.[pp] Put another way, both economic efficiency and financial feasibility can be determined without direct reference to or use of *average total costs*; thus, it is only necessary to deal with fixed costs in terms of their relationship to facility size and output capacity, and the time period in which they are committed.

To begin, the long-run objective (while assuming no intratemporal demand fluctuations and thus that flow throughout the tth time period or year, say, is constant) is to determine the investment plan which will maximize the (expected) total discounted net benefits resulting over an n year analysis period (or n year planning horizon),[qq] subject of course to the restriction that the total discounted net benefits be nonnegative.[rr] Also, as detailed throughout the preceding sections, the best pricing policy (from the standpoint of economic efficiency and maximizing total net benefits) will be to adopt marginal cost pricing.[ss] Satisfying this longer-term problem, given (just) intertemporal or year-to-year demand fluctuations, can no longer be regarded as a straightforward or deterministic problem. Rather, it probably can only be characterized as a decision-tree problem and as a problem of determining the investment action to

[pp]That is, fixed costs are not separable, and they need not and should not be allocated to specific time intervals and output levels, in contrast to variable costs which are separable.

[qq]Throughout, it is assumed that *expected* costs and benefits will be used; other strategies (such as MINIMAX and MAXIMAX) will not be considered herein.

[rr]In short, the null alternative (which will produce total discounted net benefits equal to zero) is always preferable to a plan which will result in negative total discounted net benefits, aside from social considerations.

[ss]Again, for this initial discussion the implementation of one or another pricing policy is regarded as "costless" (at least on a relative basis).

take place at the *end* of year 0, or *now* at the *start* of year 1, based on expectations of future costs and benefits and while recognizing that the costs and benefits during any future year t will be dependent or conditional upon the staging plan or actions which will be taken at the *start* of years $1, \ldots, t$.

The problem can be formulated as follows:[tt]

Let:

$$NSC(y_t|y_1, \ldots, y_{t-1}) = \text{nonseparable (fixed) costs incurred at start of year } t \text{ for plan } y_t \text{ } given \text{ that plans } y_1, \ldots, y_{t-1} \text{ were adopted in previous years} \qquad (4\text{-}30)$$

$$VC(q_t, y_t|y_1, \ldots, y_{t-1}) = \text{total variable costs incurred for output } q_t \text{ during year } t \text{ for plan } y_t|y_1, \ldots, y_{t-1} \quad (4\text{-}31)$$

$$srmc(q_t, y_t|y_1, \ldots, y_{t-1}) = \text{short-run marginal cost for output } q_t \text{ during year } t \text{ for plan } y_t|y_1, \ldots, y_{t-1} \quad (4\text{-}32)$$

$$mb_t(q_t) = \text{marginal benefit during year } t \text{ for an output or quantity demanded of } q_t. \qquad (4\text{-}33)$$

Then, for efficient utilization and maximum total net benefits during year t for plan y_t, and given the adoption of plans $y_1, \ldots, y_{t-1}$ during prior years:

$$\text{Equilibrium price } = P_t(y_t|y_1, \ldots, y_{t-1}) \qquad (4\text{-}34)$$

$$= srmc\,(Q_t, y_t|y_1, \ldots, y_{t-1}) \qquad (4\text{-}35)$$

$$= mb_t(Q_t) \quad , \qquad (4\text{-}36)$$

where

$$Q_t = \text{equilibrium flow or output during year } t \text{ for plan } y_t|y_1, \ldots, y_{t-1} \quad .$$

These equilibrium flows and prices for this simple intertemporal and linear demand case (while ignoring cross-elasticities and intratemporal fluctuations) can be determined analytically by setting the marginal benefit and short-run marginal cost expressions equal to each other and solving for the equilibrium flow (and then back-substituting to find the price). For example, using modified equations (4-2) and (2-17) for plan $y_t|y_1, \ldots, y_{t-1}$ during year t:[uu]

[tt]All demand cross-elasticities are ignored in this formulation.

[uu]Each of the parameters for the marginal cost function should be subscripted, both with respect to year t and facility plan $y_t|y_1, \ldots, y_{t-1}$, but for simplicity only part of these subscripts were used.

$$\beta_t/\alpha_t - Q_t/\alpha_t = b_y d + \frac{fdv_y}{(v_y - a_y Q_t)^2} \quad ,$$

This expression can be solved for the equilibrium flow Q_t. Then, if Q_t is back-substituted into either equation (4-2) or (2-17), the equilibrium price can be determined.

Also,

$$VC(Q_t, y_t | y_1, \ldots, y_{t-1}) = h_t \sum_{q_t=1}^{Q_t} srmc(q_t, y_t | y_1, \ldots, y_{t-1}), \qquad (4\text{-}37)$$

and

$$TB(Q_t, y_t | y_1, \ldots, y_{t-1}) = h_t \sum_{q_t=1}^{Q_t} mb_t(q_t) \qquad (4\text{-}38)$$

$$TR(Q_t, y_t | y_1, \ldots, y_{t-1}) = h_t Q_t P_t(y_t | y_1, \ldots, y_{t-1}) \quad , \qquad (4\text{-}39)$$

in which $VC( )$, $TB( )$ and $TR( )$ are the actual total variable costs, total benefits and total revenues, respectively, during the tth year for the equilibrium flow and staging plan indicated in the argument (i.e., in the parentheses); also, in these equations h_t is the number of time intervals during year t having equilibrium flow Q_t, and they assume that the flow throughout the year is constant. Consequently, if the output or flow units are trips *per hour* in year t, then the time interval would be an hour and h_t would be equal to 8760.

Also, it will be assumed (simply for computational convenience) that the marginal costs, benefits, and revenues accrue at the *end* of the year during which they are incurred or accrued (i.e., at the end of the tth year); this is in contrast to the nonseparable (or "fixed") costs which are assumed to be incurred at the *start* of year t.

Once the marginal costs, fixed costs, marginal benefits, and revenues have been enumerated—year by year for all years during the n year planning horizon, and for all plans or combinations of facility size and staging sequences—it then will be possible to reduce the costs and benefits to a comparable time base and to compare alternative facility plans and staging sequences. For this purpose, the year by year cost and benefit totals in equations (4-30) and (4-37) through (4-39) will be discounted, totalled, and compared in two ways.[vv] First, *increments* of expenditure and benefit will be compared, *working backward from year n*, to insure the economic feasibility of increments. Two, those plans for which all increments of expenditure are economically justifiable will then be compared in terms of their total net benefits discounted to the present.

To illustrate the above point, consider the simple example shown in Figure 4-10, in which only four different facility size or expansion sequencing plans are analyzed for the planning horizon of only two years (that is, *through* year two).

[vv]This procedure is outlined as a two-step procedure for computational reasons. That is, if the analysis is made incrementally—as will be detailed—the computations can be foreshortened relative to a procedure whereby *every* plan is discounted to the present.

92

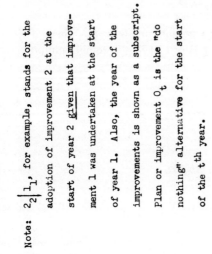

Planning Horizon is 2 Years

Note: $2_2|1_1$, for example, stands for the adoption of improvement 2 at the start of year 2 given that improvement 1 was undertaken at the start of year 1. Also, the year of the improvements is shown as a subscript. Plan or improvement 0_t is the "do nothing" alternative for the start of the tth year.

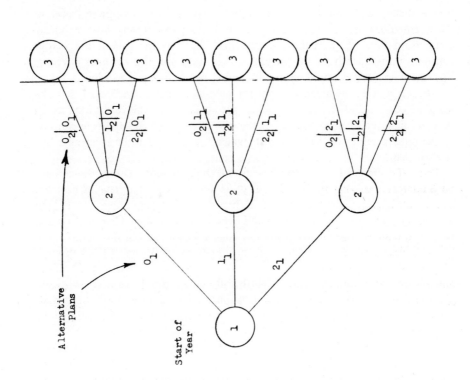

Figure 4-10. Alternative Facility and Staging Plans.

The first step of the analysis would be to examine the incremental costs and benefits from the *start* of year 2 to its end. Thus, for each of the four plans, the year 2 variable costs and benefits will be discounted to the *start* of year 2, netted, and compared with the nonseparable (or fixed) costs occurring at the start of year 2. All plans for which the incremental 2nd year benefits do not exceed the incremental 2nd year variable and fixed costs will be rejected; recall in this regard that at the end of each year throughout the planning horizon the facility can be abandoned (i.e., plan 0 can be adopted), thus reducing all future total net benefits to zero (which clearly is preferable to negative total net benefits). In turn, each of the plans which was not rejected upon examination of the last increment will be analyzed in terms of the incremental costs and benefits during the nth and $n-1$th years. The total net benefits computed before (i.e., the total net benefits discounted to the *start* of the nth year or 2nd year in this case) will be added to the benefits occurring during the $n-1$th year (and accruing at the end of the $n-1$th year); the $n-1$th year variable costs will be subtracted from these total two-year benefits, and the net will then be discounted to the start of the $n-1$th year, and then compared with the nonseparable costs (if any) which were made at the start of the $n-1$th year. Again, all plans for which the net of these benefits and costs (or total discounted net benefits for the two years) is not positive will be rejected. Finally, all plans having positive total discounted net benefits can be compared, to determine which is the most prefereable (i.e., which plan accrues the largest total discounted net benefits).

If *overall* financial feasibility for the total n-year period is also a requirement for alternative plans and projects, as might be recommended for increasing returns cases, the year by year revenues and costs *for the best plan* (i.e., for the plan having the highest total discounted net benefit) can then be discounted and totalled; if the total discounted net revenues for the best plan are positive, then both economic and financial feasibility requirements will be satisfied.

The year to year discounting (working backwards from year n) required for the incremental benefit and cost analysis can be accomplished by successively applying a one-year discount factor as follows:

$$DF_1 = \text{One-Year Discount Factor} = \frac{1}{1+i} \quad . \qquad (4\text{-}40)$$

For example, if the various benefit and cost increments for the last or nth year of the planning horizon are to be placed on a comparable time-value basis (which we will assume to be the *start* of the nth year), the total net benefits discounted to the start of year n would be as follows:

$$
\begin{aligned}
TDNB_n(y_1,\ldots,y_n) \;=\; DF_1 \Big[& TB(Q_n,y_n \,|\, y_1,\ldots,y_{n-1}) \\
& + VC(Q_n,y_n \,|\, y_1,\ldots,y_{n-1}) \Big] \\
& - NSC(y_n \,|\, y_1,\ldots,y_{n-1}) \quad , \qquad (4\text{-}41)
\end{aligned}
$$

where $TDNB_n(y_1, \ldots, y_n)$ are the total nth year net benefits discounted to the start of year n, for the staging and facility plan shown in the argument of the expression.

More generally, for carrying out the incremental analysis, the total net benefits for years t through n, when discounted to the start of year t, would be as follows:

$$
\begin{aligned}
TDNB_t(y_1, \ldots, y_n) \;=\; DF_1 \Big[& TDNB_{t+1}(y_1, \ldots, y_n) \\
& - VC(Q_t, y_t | y_1, \ldots, y_{t-1}) \\
& + TB(Q_t, y_t | y_1, \ldots, y_{t-1}) \Big] \\
& - NSC(y_t | y_1, \ldots, y_{t-1}) \quad .
\end{aligned}
\tag{4-42}
$$

For those cases in which financial feasibility is also required, the factor for discounting revenues or costs incurred or accruing at the end of the tth year would be:

$$
DF_t = \frac{1}{(1+i)^t} \quad .
\tag{4-43}
$$

Applying this factor, the total net revenues for the n year planning horizon, all discounted to the start of year 1, would be as follows (for the staging plan $y_1, \ldots, y_n$):

$$
\begin{aligned}
TDNR(y_1, \ldots, y_n) \;=\; \sum_{t=1}^{n} DF_t \Big[& TR(Q_t, y_t | y_1, \ldots, y_{t-1}) \\
& - VC(Q_t, y_t | y_1, \ldots, y_{t-1}) \\
& - NSC(y_t | y_1, \ldots, y_{t-1}) / (1+i) \Big] \quad .
\end{aligned}
\tag{4-44}
$$

The benefit-cost (or, more specifically, net present value) procedure outlined above will permit the analyst to examine the economic and financial feasibility of investments and increments of investment. Furthermore, this procedure will permit the analyst to take into account the alternatives of doing nothing now (or later), or of abandoning existing facilities at any time during the planning horizon, or of withholding expansion or investment until a later year. (Specifically, requiring increments of investment as well as the overall investment to have total discounted net benefits equal to or greater than zero implicitly accounts for these alternatives.) However, the extent to which the procedure will lead to the "optimum" investment and staging program depends on the ingenuity of engineers, planners, and designers and their ability to create "useful and worthwhile" designs, to estimate the *best* expansion plans and the best technology for providing services, and to determine the plan for which the marginal benefits just equal the marginal costs for the last increment of expenditure.

Finally, it should be noted that this procedure, *with* the accompanying pricing policy, requires the use of prices which can (and probably will) vary from year to year; the degree to which they would vary depends on the unevenness or divisibility of the technology, on demand shifts from year to year, on the staging plan, and on the nature of the plan's returns to scale (i.e., are they constant, increasing, or decreasing).

4.4.2 Intratemporal Demand Fluctuations and Efficiency

The problems of peaking or intratemporal demand fluctuations complicate investment, pricing, and efficiency planning enormously, but are of key importance. In this section both simple and complex peak-load situations will be treated, though in all cases it will be assumed that intratemporal (or hour-to-hour) demand functions remain constant from day to day and from year to year; also, intratemporal demand *cross*-elasticities will be ignored.

The first case to be discussed will be that in which the demand fluctuations during the day can be characterized by just two demand functions, one for the demand during n_p peak-load hours and a second for the demand during n_o off-peak-load hours;[ww] the demand during each hour of the peak-period will be identical, and that during each off-peak period hour will be identical. Also, for this first case, it will be assumed that the long-run marginal cost is constant; further, it will be assumed that the short-run marginal cost functions (and thus total variable cost functions) for different levels of capacity or facility size, differ from one another only by a horizontal translation. All of these features are illustrated in Figure 4-11, with cost curves being shown for facility sizes y and z.

The relationships on Figure 4-11 do not directly permit assessment of the economic feasibility of either facility y or z or of that for the increment from y to z. This follows, since the *lrmc* curve applies only for facilities which have constant output levels, for which the short-run and long-run marginal costs are identical, hardly the case here; also, no account is taken of changes in fixed costs. While it is evident that for whatever facility selected economic efficiency can be maximized (that is, total net benefits will be largest) when short-run marginal cost pricing is employed, the total net benefits will not necessarily be positive.

[ww]This does not imply that the peak-period must consist of n_p *consecutive* hours, however; for example, if n_p were five hours, the morning peak load could be two hours long and the afternoon peak load could be three hours long, with each peak-load hour having the same demand and equilibrium flow.

For any facility y, the daily total net benefits can be computed as follows, when there are r different demand periods:[xx]

$$TNB_y = \sum_{x=1}^{r} n_x \sum_{q=1}^{q_{x,y}} \left[mb_x(q) - srmc_y(q) \right] - 24F_y \quad , (4\text{-}45)$$

where F_y is the hourly fixed cost for facility y, $mb_x(q)$ is the marginal benefit during the xth demand period for a flow of q, and $q_{x,y}$ is the equilibrium flow (under short-run marginal cost pricing) for the xth demand period with facility y, and n_x is the number of hours in the xth demand period. Also, the "optimum" facility can be determined by incrementally increasing the facility size, so long as the incremental total net benefit is equal to or greater than zero. The incremental total net benefit associated with increasing the facility size from level y to z is as follows:

$$ITNB_{yz} = \Delta TNB_{yz} = TNB_z - TNB_y$$
$$= \sum_{x=1}^{r} n_x \sum_{q=q_{x,y}}^{q_{x,z}} mb_x(q) - 24(F_z - F_y)$$
$$- \sum_{x=1}^{r} n_x \left[VC_z(q_{x,z}) - VC_y(q_{x,y}) \right] \quad , \qquad (4\text{-}46)$$

where $VC_y(q_{x,y})$ is the hourly variable cost for facility y during the xth demand period when the hourly flow is $q_{x,y}$.

In situations of perfect divisibility, capacity would be continually expanded until the incremental total net benefit (for the last unit of output added), as calculated by equation (4-46), was equal to zero; otherwise, facilities would be expanded so long as the incremental total net benefit continued to be nonnegative.

With short-run marginal cost pricing, equilibrium conditions for the yth facility during the xth demand period would occur when the following conditions hold:

Equilibrium price $= p(q_{x,y})$
$$= srmc_y(q_{x,y})$$
$$= mb_x(q_{x,y}) \quad ,$$

[xx]The xth demand period includes n_x hours of equal hourly flow. Also, for facility y, the optimum output level for constant hourly flow throughout the day is q_y. Further, this formulation of total net benefit applies regardless of whether there are constant, increasing, or decreasing returns to scale.

97

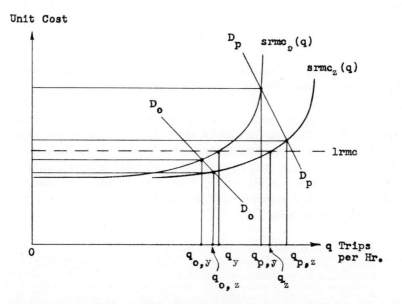

Unit Cost

Figure 4-11. Cost and Demand Relationships for Two-Period Intratemporal Demand and Two Facility Sizes.

where $q_{x,y}$ and $p(q_{x,y})$ are the equilibrium flow and equilibrium price, respectively, during the xth demand period for the yth facility.

For marginal cost and benefit relationships such as are shown in Figure 4-11, it is clear that uniform prices set equal to $p(q_{x,y}) = srmc_y(q_{x,y})$ would produce both benefits and revenues in excess of the total variable costs for the total daily flow; this would hold true since the marginal costs are always rising, and therefore the average variable costs must be lower than marginal costs and prices during all r demand periods. It will also have to be shown, though, that the excess benefit exceeds the fixed costs for facility y; that is, in order to demonstrate economic feasibility one only need show that:

$$\sum_{x=1}^{r} n_x \sum_{q=1}^{q_{x,y}} \left[mb_x(q) - srmc_y(q) \right] \geqslant 24F_y \quad .$$

For financial feasibility as well, the following additional condition must also hold:

$$\sum_{x=1}^{r} n_x \left[q_{x,y} p(q_{x,y}) - VC_y(q_{x,y}) \right] \geqslant 24F_y$$

or

$$\sum_{x=1}^{r} n_x q_{x,y} \left[p(q_{x,y}) - \mathit{sravc}_y(q_{x,y}) \right] \geqslant 24F_y \quad .$$

The work of M. Boiteux of France on the subject of peak-load pricing deals with the above differential pricing problem, among other key matters.[7] According to Boiteux, the facility of optimum scale or capacity (for situations with periodic loads or, say, with peak and off-peak demand functions such as are shown in Figure 4-11) is the one for which the total costs for the equilibrium peak and off-peak flows will be minimized (under short-run marginal cost pricing and while clearing the market, etc.);[8] this objective function clearly is much different from that outlined earlier. From this, Boiteux concluded that for "optimum" facility capacity and for short-run marginal cost pricing the following condition holds:[9]

$$\sum_{x=1}^{r} n_x \mathit{srmc}_y(q_{x,y}) = \mathit{lrmc} \sum_{x=1}^{r} n_x \quad . \tag{4-47}$$

However, Boiteux noted that this condition applies only ". . . when the development [or long-run marginal] cost is constant and the expenditure [or total cost] curves for plants of various capacities are congruent and differ only in position. If the outputs [or equilibrium flows] are not very different or if the $[LRTC_y(q)]$ curves do not alter shape greatly when the capacity of the plant is changed, the formula holds as a first approximation."[10]

For the Boiteux solution, the tolls for the optimum facility y would be equal to the difference of short-run marginal costs and the short-run average variable costs (assuming, again, that short-run average variable costs are equivalent to the perceived travel payments); thus, for an hour during the xth demand period the toll for facility y would be:

$$T_{x,y} = \mathit{srmc}_y(q_{x,y}) - \mathit{sravcy}(q_{x,y}) \quad . \tag{4-48}$$

While this particular solution insures that the total payment by tripmakers (tolls plus average variable or perceived travel costs) would just equal the total *variable* costs[yy] for the "optimum" facility, *if* it were operated at its "optimum" flow level at all times (which it does not), it does not insure that the total net benefits are positive, that the total net revenues are positive, or that the total toll revenues at least equal the fixed facility costs. Thus, while total net benefits are maximized (by virtue of short-run marginal cost pricing), neither economic nor financial feasibility is assured.[11]

[yy]For this constant long-run marginal cost case, total costs rather than total *variable* costs would be appropriate here, *if* there were constant returns to scale.

Finally, from the foregoing remarks which summarize some aspects of peak-load pricing, it should be apparent that no straightforward deterministic method exists for determining either the "optimum" facility size, or the consequences with respect to economic or financial feasibility, even without considering intertemporal demand fluctuations. Rather, in much the same fashion as indicated in subsection (4.4.1), it will be necessary for the analyst to specify the various alternatives to be considered, to determine equilibrium flow and price levels (under, say, marginal cost pricing) and in turn the total net benefits for each, according to equation (4-45). All facility designs having negative total net benefits will be rejected, and that one having the highest nonnegative total net benefit will be selected as the most desirable in terms of economic feasibility and efficiency. However, if the total toll revenues for that facility, using marginal cost pricing and tolls set according to equation (4-48), do not produce revenues at least as large as the total fixed facility costs, then financial infeasibility will result for the agency in question (whether public or private).

4.4.3 Joint Consideration of Intertemporal and Intratemporal Demand Fluctuations

In most instances, the analyst will find it necessary to take account of both inter- and intratemporal demand fluctuations in his search for the "optimal" investment and staging plan. To undertake such an assignment, there seems to be little doubt that a benefit-cost analysis and decision-tree approach, comparable to that outlined for the intertemporal situation in subsection (4.4.1), would be most suitable.

The outline of the procedure would be as follows:

$NSC(y_t|y_1,\ldots,y_{t-1}) =$ nonseparable (fixed) costs incurred at start of year t for plan y_t *given* that plans $y_1,\ldots,y_{t-1}$ were adopted in previous years $\qquad$ (4-49)

$VC(q_{x,t},y_t|y_1,\ldots,y_{t-1}) =$ total variable costs for flow $q_{x,t}$ during the xth demand period of year t for plan $y_t|y_1,\ldots,y_{t-1}$ $\qquad$ (4-50)

$srmc(q_{x,t},y_t|y_1,\ldots,y_{t-1}) =$ short-run marginal cost for output $q_{x,t}$ during the xth demand period of year t for plan $y_t|y_1,\ldots,y_{t-1}$ $\qquad$ (4-51)

$mb(q_{x,t})$ = marginal benefit for output $q_{x,t}$ during the xth demand
period for year t for plan $y_t | y_1, \ldots, y_{t-1}$.   (4-52)

For most efficient utilization and maximum net benefits during the xth demand period of year t for plan y_t, given the adoption of plans $y_1, \ldots, y_{t-1}$ during previous years, the following conditions must hold:

$$\text{Equilibrium price} = P_{x,t}(y_t | y_1, \ldots, y_{t-1}) \qquad (4\text{-}53)$$

$$= srmc\,(Q_{x,t}, y_t | y_1, \ldots, y_{t-1}) \qquad (4\text{-}54)$$

$$= mb_t\,(Q_{x,t}) \quad , \qquad (4\text{-}55)$$

where
$Q_{x,t}$ = equilibrium flow or output during xth demand period of
year t for plan $y_t | y_1, \ldots, y_{t-1}$.

As before, the equilibrium flow and price can be determined analytically (while ignoring cross-elasticities)[12] by setting the marginal benefit and short-run marginal cost expressions equal to each other. For example, modifying equations (4-2) and (2-17), for plan $y_t | y_1, \ldots, y_{t-1}$ and for the xth demand period in year t:[zz]

$$\beta_{x,t}/\alpha_{x,t} - Q_{x,t}/\alpha_{x,t} = b_y d + \frac{fd v_y}{(v_y - a_y Q_{x,t})^2} \; ; \qquad (4\text{-}56)$$

this expression can be solved for the equilibrium flow, $Q_{x,t}$, a value which can then be back-substituted into either the marginal benefit or marginal cost expression to determine the equilibrium price.

Further,

$$VC(Q_t, y_t | y_1, \ldots, y_{t-1}) = h_t \sum_{x=1}^{r} n_x \sum_{q_{x,t}=1}^{Q_{x,t}} srmc(q_{x,t}, y_t | y_1, \ldots, y_{t-1}) \; . \qquad (4\text{-}57)$$

and

$$TB(Q_t, y_t | y_1, \ldots, y_{t-1}) = h_t \sum_{x=1}^{r} n_x \sum_{q_{x,t}=1}^{Q_{x,t}} mb_t(q_{x,t}) \qquad (4\text{-}58)$$

[zz]Each of the parameters for the marginal cost function should be subscripted both for the year and facility plan; but for simplicity, only part of these subscripts were used.

$$TR(Q_t, y_t | y_1, \ldots, y_{t-1}) = h_x \sum_{x=1}^{r} n_x Q_{x,t} P_{x,t}(y_t | y_1, \ldots, y_{t-1}) \quad , \quad (4\text{-}59)$$

in which $VC(\ )$, $TB(\ )$ and $TR(\ )$ are the actual total variable costs, total benefits, and total revenues during all r demand periods of year t for the staging plan indicated in the argument; Q_t is a variable to represent equilibrium flow during the year t. Also, n_x is the number of time intervals in the xth demand period, with each interval having flow $Q_{x,t}$, and h_t is the number of identical demand periods occurring during the year t. Consequently, if the output units are trips per hour, then n_x would be the number of hours (during a day) having a flow $Q_{x,t}$ and the sum of n_x over all x (i.e., $x = 1, \ldots, r$) would be 24; if all days during the year t had an identical set of demand functions, h_t would be equal to 365.

From here on out, the analysis of the total net benefits (or total net revenues) and treatment of year by year discounting and incremental affects will be identical to that outlined in subsection (4.4.1). The formulas, shown earlier in equations (4-40) through (4-44), are entirely applicable to the joint intra-temporal and intertemporal $VC(\ )$, $TB(\ )$, $TR(\ )$, and $NSC(\ )$ expressions shown in equations (4-57) through (4-59) plus (4-49), and require no changes in notation or subscripts. Thus the methods and equations need not be repeated.

4.5 Concluding Remarks

The earlier sections of this chapter outlined the interactions between cost, demand, and pricing under very idealized circumstances, but nonetheless provided a somewhat general framework to guide the designer and planner in his search for better designs and technologies. Furthermore, in these introductory remarks, the conflict between economic efficiency and financial feasibility which can exist was noted, along with some of the reasons for permitting one aspect or another to override.

However, once it becomes necessary to account for the demand fluctuations that invariably exist, either intertemporally (year to year) or intratemporally (hour to hour or season to season), or both, the last of which is usually the case, the idealized and deterministic structure for decision-making on questions of the best investment and output level does not appear suitable. Rather, in its stead, it becomes necessary to detail particular plans, and to analyze their consequences on the more usual benefit-cost basis. The details of this type of analysis have been included to permit full accounting of the time-value aspects, as well as intratemporal and intertemporal demand fluctuations (while ignoring cross-elasticities). No attempt was made to justify the particular discounting and benefit-cost procedure which was outlined, because of its wide coverage elsewhere in the literature. Finally, it should be noted that feasibility analysis was mainly considered in this chapter for marginal cost pricing, though some of the ramifications stemming from other policies was noted. Further, no note was made of the practical difficulties or costs of implementing such a pricing policy or of the distributional aspects involved. These issues will be touched upon in Chapter 5.

5

Investment Planning and Pricing in Practice

Thus far the subjects of investment planning and of economic and financial feasibility have been explored under a very strict set of economic conditions, which admittedly are at variance with the "real world" situation. Therefore, it will be useful to reexamine some of the earlier conclusions, in light of some of these differences, and to outline how the investment planning and decision-making process would thereby be altered.

Among the aspects to be discussed in more detail are: (1) implementation of differential or peak-load pricing;[a] (2) consistency of benefit-cost analysis between the private and public sectors; (3) difficulties of measuring consumer surplus; (4) matters of cost and benefit incidence; (5) specification of output units and equilibrium; and (6) nonhomogeneous privately-perceived travel costs. It should be noted that these matters will, for the most part, be discussed in abbreviated form and in general rather than in specific terms.

5.1 Problems and Practicalities of Utilizing Differential (or Peak Load) Pricing Versus Uniform Tax Pricing[1]

On the one hand, and for reasons of economic efficiency, the utilization of perfectly differentiated pricing systems and of different prices from hour to hour can be argued in order to assure that prices are matched exactly to the actual short-run marginal costs, and that total net benefits are maximized; one might argue that pricing of this sort would be ideal and lead to the best allocation of resources, both from hour to hour and from year to year. On the other hand, the existence of different hour-to-hour, day-to-day, week-to-week, and season-to-season demand functions and the high cost of implementing price differentiation to account for all these differences argue against its implementation, as a practical matter.

As a consequence, less than "perfectly" differentiated pricing policies must be considered; among other possibilities, these can include uniform taxes, uniform tolls, simple peak and off-peak differential tolls, or more highly differentiated rate structures with tolls varying during, say, three or more periods of the day and from season to season. Invariably, each of these pricing schemes involves price discrimination or subsidy of one sort or another, and

---

[a]The terms "peak-load pricing," "differential pricing," and "marginal cost pricing" will be used interchangeably throughout this chapter.

103

necessitates departure from the idealized conditions under which optimal efficiency can theoretically be anticipated. Thus, the benefits and costs of these pricing possibilities will have to be examined and compared in order to make any statements regarding the most appropriate alternative.

To examine the effects of instituting different pricing policies, the circumstances will be explored in detail for two cases, one in which a uniform user tax is imposed, and the second, in which differential or so-called peak-load tolls are employed. Differential tolls may be used to implement short-run marginal cost pricing, while uniform user taxes are usually applied for financial reasons. For this initial analysis and comparison, let us assume that demand can be fully represented by a pair of peak and off-peak demand functions, and that no other diurnal, seasonal, or year-to-year fluctuations occur; and, as before, it will be assumed that the privately perceived travel costs are equal to the short-run average variable costs, or $sravc_z(q)$, *exclusive* of any user taxes or tolls.

For analyzing the consequences of imposing uniform user taxes, relative to those for *costless* marginal cost pricing,[b] the demand and cost relationships shown in Figure 5-1 (for some facility z) will be used. The $srmc_z(q)$ and $sravc_z(q)$ curves are as described previously (and include all costs for the facility and vehicles operating thereon, as well as all personal travel time and effort costs, exclusive of any user tax or toll); the $srtvc_z(q)$ curve is equal to the privately perceived travel costs *including* the uniform tax, and thus is equal to $sravc_z(q)$ *plus* the uniform user tax.[c]

For this two-period demand case, perfect price differentiation *and* maximization of total net benefits would be effected by charging $p(q_p)$ during peak hours and $p(q_o)$ during off-peak hours—*so long as the costs of implementing differential prices and collecting the fees or tolls are excluded.*[d] (Before considering the effects of including the toll collection and implementation costs, the consequences of a uniform tax pricing policy, relative to those for "costless" marginal cost pricing, will first be analyzed.) The equilibrium prices and flows for peak and off-peak periods, which would result from differential or marginal cost pricing, would differ considerably from those resulting from the use of short-run average variable costs combined with uniform user taxes. The latter policy is similar to that now in practice for the great bulk of U.S. public roads and streets; the $srtvc_z(q)$ curve on Figure 5-1 illustrates the price-volume function for this type of policy.[e] This policy would result in "underutilization" of the facility for

---

[b]By *costless*, it is meant, not including the costs of *or* caused by collecting tolls.

[c]This uniform tax can be set on any basis desired; however, if financial feasibility is desired, the tax can be determined and set according to the model outlined in Chapter 3, equations (3-4) through (3-7).

[d]These costs will include the commitments for whatever facilities may be required (toll gates, auditing equipment, monitors, etc.), the cost of operating the facilities, collecting tolls, auditing, etc., *as well as* the not insignificant costs of any added delays (or accidents, etc.) to the travelers while they pay the toll.

[e]For the purposes of this analysis, it will be assumed that the user taxes are perfectly uniform, and do not vary with amount of vehicular use or with the volume on a facility. This latter assumption is clearly wrong, since gasoline consumption varies with vehicular speed and frequency of slowdowns or stops.

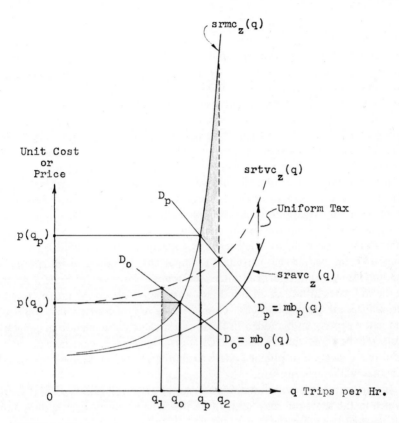

Figure 5-1. Short-Run Cost, Demand, and Pricing Relationships for Uniform User Tax Pricing Policy.

equilibrium flows below the point where $srtvc_z(q)$ is equal to $srmc_z(q)$, and in "overutilization" for flows above (relative, of course, to a policy of "costless" short-run marginal cost pricing). Thus, for uniform tax and variable cost pricing, net benefits would be foregone to the extent of the shaded area to the left of q_o, and net costs (or relative losses) would be incurred to the extent of the shaded area to the right of q_p *plus* any costs for collecting user taxes. The daily loss in total net benefits for average variable cost plus uniform tax pricing (relative to "costless" marginal cost pricing) would be:

$$\text{A.V.C. Relative Loss} = n_o \sum_{q=q_1}^{q_o} \left[mb_o(q) - srmc_z(q) \right]$$

$$+ n_p \sum_{q=q_p}^{q_2} \left[srmc_z(q) - mb_p(q) \right]$$

$$+ \text{ Collection Costs,} \qquad\qquad (5\text{-}1)$$

where n_o and n_p are the number of hours of off-peak and peak period flow, respectively. *It is important to emphasize, however, that the collection costs for uniform user gas or fuel taxes are extremely small (negligible for all intents and purposes) and are simple to administer;*[f] these are the principal virtues of employing such a pricing policy, at least as an economic efficiency matter.[g]

However, the problem is not as straightforward with respect to the implementation of a peak-load or marginal cost pricing policy, in which prices differ from hour to hour or as marginal costs vary. First, there are a wide number of possible mechanisms and devices which can be used to implement such a policy, varying from taxes imposed at the destination end of the trip, to parking imposts, vehicle meters, electronic devices, special licenses, and toll gates.[2] Second, for these sorts of situations (and certainly any scheme involving toll gates or equipment and having toll facility costs which do not vary with output in the short-run), it is vital to consider the collection cost possibilities over the long-run; this would be particularly important in toll gate situations, for example, since in the short-run, increased input volume can increase congestion at the toll gates in no less an important way than it can on the facility to which the vehicles are gaining entrance. Over the long-run, of course, more toll booths and gate keepers can be added in those cases where the reduction in congestion costs will be more than offsetting. Of course, long-run circumstances will vary from one collection or pricing system to another, but the principles for planning purposes will remain the same.

In Figure 5-2, the cost functions are shown for a toll-gate type of operation (which in the short-run may seem to be the most costly type of system, but is not necessarily so over the long-run[h]); also, let us assume that the number of toll gates and gatekeepers being utilized represents the long-run "optimum" for the demand and cost conditions portrayed here. The $srmc_z'(q)$ and $sravc_z'(q)$ curves, respectively, are the short-run marginal cost and short-run average variable costs for facility z, *including* the variable toll collection costs and traveler delays (and increased vehicle operating costs, etc.) which result from using differential tolls

---

[f]This statement is reasonable at present and for internal combustion engines, but would probably not be true for large-scale adoption of battery-operated or electric automobiles. With the advent of battery-operated automobiles, a more complex and costly type of pricing setup probably would be required.

[g]They have other virtues, however, especially as revenue raising mechanisms. Since highway travel (in vehicle-miles) is so large, and since demand is very price inelastic with respect to gas and other user taxes (at least for present levels), they serve as excellent tools for providing enormously high levels of revenue, and thus for financing heavy investments (purely aside from the matter of whether they are economically efficient or not).

[h]For example, vehicle meters or electronic monitoring devices may have quite low short-run marginal and average variable costs, but over the long-run, may well have capital and maintenance costs (etc.) which exceed those for this seemingly more expensive toll-gate technology.

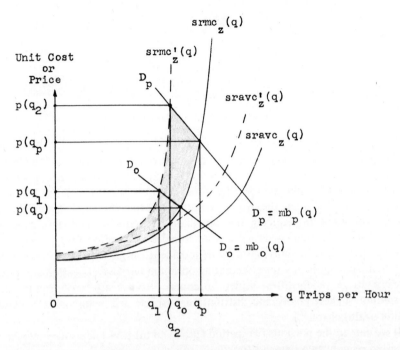

Figure 5-2. Short-Run Cost, Demand, and Pricing Relationships for Peak-Load or Marginal Cost Pricing.

and toll gates to implement a peak-load or marginal cost pricing policy. Relative to the "costless" marginal cost pricing situation, as represented by $srmc_z(q)$, facility z will be underutilized for all levels of output, and the relative loss in net benefit during peak hours will be equal to the entire shaded area shown in Figure 5-2, and during off-peak hours will be equal to the shaded area lying below the off-peak demand function (D_o). Mathematically, the daily loss in total net benefit for marginal cost pricing, to include toll collection costs and those travel delays while tolls are being collected (relative to "costless" marginal cost pricing), will be as follows:

$$\text{M.C. Relative Loss} = n_o \sum_{q=1}^{q_1} \left[srmc_z'(q) - srmc_z(q) \right]$$

$$+ n_o \sum_{q=q_1}^{q_o} \left[mb_o(q) - srmc_z(q) \right]$$

$$+ n_p \sum_{q=1}^{q_2} \left[srmc_z'(q) - srmc_z(q) \right]$$

$$+ n_p \sum_{q=q_2}^{q_p} \left[mb_p(q) - srmc_z(q) \right]$$

$$+ \text{Fixed Toll Collection Costs} \qquad . \qquad (5\text{-}2)$$

The relative loss in net benefit from using differential tolls to implement marginal cost pricing is *not necessarily* less than the relative loss from using average variable cost plus uniform tax pricing; that is, the M.C. relative loss may or may not be less than the A.V.C. relative loss. In some cases, marginal cost pricing will result in reducing the overall net benefits (everything else being equal), and in reducing economic efficiency more than uniform tax pricing, and in other cases, less. In short, no *a priori* judgment can be made with respect to the "best" pricing policy for effectuating optimum resource allocation and most efficient usage of facilities, aside, of course, from matters of equity and distribution. (These equity and distributional aspects will be discussed in a later section of this chapter.)

If we extend the previous two-period (peak and off-peak) demand case, which consisted of only two demand functions, to a more realistic demand representation, as many as twenty-four time-of-day demand functions can be required (if the time interval for output were one hour and if it seems reasonable to ignore the differences in minute-to-minute flow rates and travel costs within an hourly period); thus, as many as twenty-four hourly toll rates would be required if "perfect" price differentiation and marginal cost pricing were to be employed. The use of twenty-four different rates, even in situations of stable demand, would result in some degree of disequilibrium and, probably, in less than the "optimum" or at least the desired results; this would be even more pronounced if the directional characteristics were taken into account (and thus if forty-eight different demand functions and toll rates were employed).[i] On the other hand, the information needs and system analyses required to fully characterize the forty-eight demand functions, and to properly determine rates by hour and by direction, may be so costly (in terms of data gathering, processing, and analysis), and the resulting rate and flow conditions so complex, as to suggest the "desirability" of less than "perfectly differentiated" pricing. That is, for the above reasons, it may be appropriate to simulate the demand conditions by only approximate relationships for groups of hours (such as three or four demand

---

[i]Unless reversible lanes, controls, or other devices were used to maintain fairly equal flow rates (and thus marginal costs) in the two directions of flow for double-barrel facilities, it is reasonably clear that directional rates should be used for radial type facilities on which traffic is strongly unbalanced during peak periods.

109

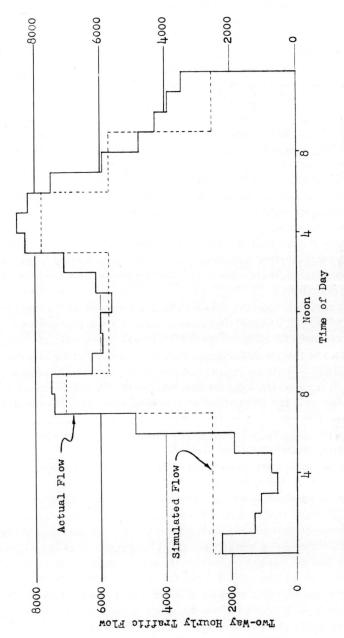

Figure 5-3. Actual and Simulated Two-Way Hourly Flow on Lodge-Ford Expressway.

functions, each of which can represent the demand during more than one hour during the day), and to use only three or four toll rates during the 24-hour day.

Figure 5-3 shows a rough means of verifying the extent to which daily demand and equilibrium flow may be approximated by grouping hours and by using just four demand periods. The simulated equilibrium flow was obtained from the model outlined in equations (3-4) through (3-7) and using the coefficients outlined in Appendix 3; this situation corresponds to the conditions on the Lodge-Ford Expressway, the actual flow for which was as shown in Figure 5-3.[j] It can be observed from this figure that the largest distortions occur during the late evening and early morning hours, when the simulated equilibrium flow is about 2600 hourly trips; however, the distortion in costs or in the value of $srtvc_z(q)$, which results from understating the flow between midnight and 7 A.M. and from overstating the flow between 9 P.M. and midnight, is small. To be more specific (and referring to the average variable cost linearizations shown in Figure 3-9), the simulated equilibrium cost is about 63 cents plus 2 cents tax for the 5-mile trip during all the above 10 hours, while the actual cost varied between 59 and 70 cents (including tax) for the 5-mile trips; in short, the flow levels during these hours were such that congestion and travel costs were increasing only slightly.

Two conclusions might be drawn from this discussion of the more realistic and highly variant demand fluctuations. One, total net benefits should be analyzed not only for different staging plans and facility sizes (as outlined in Chapter 4), but also for different pricing policies and collection schemes. Two, among the different pricing policies and collection schemes to be considered and evaluated in terms of the total net benefits, one should include various types of uniform tax and fee alternatives and various types of differential pricing alternatives. For the latter, it would be appropriate to include a "perfectly" differentiated scheme with different rates for each hour of day and direction, as well as schemes with some degree of aggregation and with more stable rates; aggregated versions might differentiate merely by peak and off-peak flows and by direction. Also, for each of the differentiated pricing schemes, it might be reasonable to evaluate the use of uniform taxes, which could then serve as a form of toll during the "base period," or period having lowest price, and require differentials to be charged only during the other hours of the day. For example, referring to Figure 5-3, a uniform tax could be imposed on all flow (by use of a gasoline or fuel tax, say), and could be set to serve as the "base period" toll for flow during the 10-hour period from 9 P.M. to 7 A.M.; then the difference between the marginal cost and average variable cost plus uniform tax could be charged during the remainder of the day. Thus, toll gate operations (if that were the price differentiation method used) would be required for only 14 hours a day, saving considerably in collection costs.

---

[j]For this particular facility, the average variable cost plus uniform tax model or $srtvc_z(q)$ is appropriate for representing the price-volume function.

The earlier benefit-cost analysis procedure outlined in subsection (4.4.3) of Chapter 4 can be modified to take account of the pricing policy as follows:

1. Let y_t represent the facility plan size *and* pricing policy adopted for year t; thus, all of the definitions shown in equations (4-49) through (4-52) will also apply here, except that any nonseparable and variable costs resulting from the pricing policy or toll collection method will also have to be included. Notationally, to indicate that all facility, travel, *and* toll collection costs are included, the symbols for equations (4-49), (4-50), and (4-51)—the fixed, total variable and short-run marginal costs—will be changed to $NSC'($ $)$, $VC'($ $)$, and $srmc'$ $($ $)$ respectively (i.e., "primes" will be added).

2. The determination of the equilibrium flow and price during the xth demand period of year t for plan and pricing policy $y_t|y_1, \ldots, y_{t-1}$ will of course depend both on the demand function and price-volume function (where the latter is dependent both on the facility plan and pricing policy). The equilibrium conditions for just two possible pricing policies may be outlined as follows:

(a)   *Average Variable Cost plus Uniform Tax Pricing:*[k]

$$\text{Equilibrium price} = P_{x,t}(y_t|y_1, \ldots y_{t-1}) \tag{5-3}$$

$$= sravc(Q_{x,t}, y_t|y_1, \ldots, y_{t-1})$$

$$+ T_{y,t} \tag{5-4}$$

$$= mb_t(Q_{x,t}) \tag{5-5}$$

where $T_{y,t}$ is the uniform tax in year t for the plan and pricing policy $y_t|y_1, \ldots, y_{t-1}$, $sravc($ $)$ is the short-run average variable cost exclusive of the user tax (which is assumed to be equivalent to perceived user travel costs, excluding user taxes), and the other symbols are as defined previously. If we assume that the demand functions are linear and that the collection costs are negligible, equations (4-2) and 2-15) can be modified so that the equilibrium flow and price (or short-run average variable cost plus uniform tax) can be determined; thus[l]

$$\beta_{x,t}/\alpha_{x,t} - Q_{x,t}/\alpha_{x,t} = b_y d + \frac{fd}{v_y - a_y Q_{x,t}} + T_{y,t} \; ; \tag{5-6}$$

this expression can be used to solve for the equilibrium flow $Q_{x,t}$, a value which can be back-substituted into the marginal benefit equation to determine the equilibrium price $P_{x,t}($ $)$. Or,

---

[k]For the present, we will not be concerned with how the uniform tax is or "should" be determined or related to costs (if that is to be done).

[l]As before, demand cross-elasticities are ignored in this expression.

$$P_{x,t}(y_t \mid y_1, \ldots, y_{t-1}) = \beta_{x,t}/\alpha_{x,t} \quad -Q_{x,t}/a_{x,t}. \tag{5-7}$$

(b)   *Short-run Marginal Cost Pricing during All Demand Periods:*

$$\text{Equilibrium price} = P_{x,t}(y_t \mid y_1, \ldots, y_{t-1} \tag{5-8}$$

$$= srmc'(Q_{x,t}, y_t \mid t_1, \ldots, y_{t-1} \tag{5-9}$$

$$= mb_t(Q_{x,t}) \quad , \tag{5-10}$$

where $srmc'(\ )$ is the short-run marginal cost for flow $Q_{x,t}$ during the xth demand period of year t for $y_t \mid y_1, \ldots, y_{t-1}$ *including* the additional facility and traveler costs which are incurred for and during toll collection. $T_{x,y,t}$, the toll charged during the xth demand period of year t for the plan and pricing policy $y_t \mid y_1, \ldots, y_{t-1}$, is:

$$T_{x,y,t} = srmc'(Q_{x,t}, y_t \mid y_1, \ldots, y_{t-1})$$
$$-sravc' (Q_{x,t}, y_t \mid y_1, \ldots, y_{t-1}) \quad . \tag{5-11}$$

In the above expression, it is implicitly assumed that all (or virtually all) of the variable toll collection costs are incurred directly by travelers, and are perceived by them in their tripmaking calculus.[m]

A final comment is in order with respect to the year-to-year fluctuation of toll rates which results either from changes in facility size at various stages of development or from changes in demand or technological conditions. On this matter, Boiteux has summarized the issues in the following way:[3]

Plant may be of unsuitable capacity for various reasons—unintentional over-equipment through erroneous forecasting, unintentional lag in equipment through underestimating the anticipated expansion of demand or owing to shortages of materials, or deliberate overequipment in anticipation of a sub-sequent development of demand. Under the marginal theory it would be necessary to fix rates at the differential cost all the time [that is, the rate would be equal to the short-run marginal cost of the particular plant in existence at each point in time], so that the optimum use is made of the plant as it stands. But the need to keep rates steady (which has nothing to do with the marginal theory) makes long-term policy preferable to the *instantaneous* optimum use of investment; the underlying principle of this is to fix rates equivalent to what the differential *[or short-run marginal] costs would be if the plant were constantly at correct capacity*, that is, rates equivalent to the development [or long-run marginal] costs.

5.2 Consistent Allocation Practices Between and Within the Public and Private Sectors

In Chapter 4, the discussion dealt with problems which can arise in increasing returns to scale (or falling average cost) situations. It was noted, in brief, that in

---

[m]Obviously, then, all of the costs incurred to provide the toll collection facilities and to operate them are assumed to be fixed. Of course, in a strict interpretation of the "short-run," this would be correct.

such instances marginal cost pricing (with a single price) could lead to the adoption of projects which would result in financial deficits, and thus require subsidies. Also, it was pointed out that failure to adopt all public and private projects falling into this category could result in allocation distortions between the public and private sectors (even aside from other market imperfections which distort allocation).

With regard to these matters, a conservative view was taken, and it was suggested that one *might* conclude that only those public investments having maximum (positive) total net benefit, and nonnegative total net revenue (i.e., those being most efficient economically and having financial feasibility) should be undertaken. This view was based on intuitive feelings about the importance of treating public and private investments consistently, and on the difficulty of measuring consumer surplus, rather than on any well-defined knowledge about the relative or absolute consequences of excluding or including consumer surplus.[4]

Perhaps the simplest and principal reason for excluding consumer surplus can best be summarized by a statement of Edward Renshaw, made in reference to navigation project benefit measurement.[5]

If the full amount of the estimated consumer surplus were used to justify public expenditures in a one-to-one benefit-cost ratio (fulfilling the requirement imposed by law that benefits equal or exceed costs), there would exist no real social surplus associated with navigation investment. Use of the entire surplus to justify public investment in navigation might, therefore, leave nothing to balance alternative real surpluses which might be associated with the same funds invested in industries which are unable to collect surpluses.

To the contrary, however, *if* there were sufficient reason to believe that decreasing returns to scale projects or programs usually fell *just* within the public sector, there would be good reason to delete the financial feasibility requirement. (At the present time, though, there appears to be little reason to suspect that this assumption is valid; the railroad industry alone serves to contradict such a view.) The requirement of financial feasibility for public projects is also weakened by the existence of private industries which tend to produce at the optimum scale even in falling cost situations, making up the financial losses (which otherwise would occur) by price discrimination or cross-subsidy of one sort or another.

The "proper" treatment of external costs and benefits is another difficult aspect when attempting to insure consistency between public and private investment programs. Earlier, it was suggested that government agencies tend to be more concerned with external benefits, than with external benefits *and* costs, and that they usually fail to treat public and private projects in like manner. Furthermore, the possibility, if not probability, of double-counting with respect to external benefits or of including improper benefit items (such as loss in tax revenues) is a cause for continual concern with government sponsored programs.[6]

→ However, it is clear that *all* externalities *should* be taken into account for all public projects, even for those instances in which the public and private sectors cannot be treated in like manner. In this respect, the problem is to insure that benefit-cost analyses within the public sector are complete and unbiased. A second problem is to develop the estimation and evaluation methodology which will permit externalities to be properly handled for both sectors and which will insure appropriate resource allocation between the two.

Of course, there are enormous difficulties at the present time in determining appropriate values for the external effects (of public or private projects)—such as those for air pollution, noise and sonic booms, involuntary displacement or property acquisition, nontransport property damage, nontransport personal injury or loss of life. Between determining values for external costs and benefits, it appears that finding appropriate values for external benefits is much more elusive and difficult. One possibility for determining external costs was mentioned earlier; it was to determine the costs which would be required to reduce the external effects to, say, a "tolerable" or "negligible" level. For example, what would be the incremental cost of designing and operating vehicles, such that they would emit toxic fumes and pollutants of only a "tolerable" amount or below; or, what would be the incremental cost of locating highways either on different alignments or below the surface, thus reducing noise levels or displacement and property acquisition to levels of public "indifference". Certainly, such a procedure hinges on one's judgment of what is "tolerable," and could easily overstate or understate the actual external consequences, and thus provide less than an adequate measure. Alternatively, one could adopt regulatory procedures which would require voluntary settlement between the operating agency (or firm) and all disadvantaged parties, and require agreement upon suitable compensation for the external damages; these damage payments (some would be lump-sum, one-time payments and others would be of a variable nature) would, in turn, enter the usual cost and pricing calculus and benefit-cost analysis.[n] Once a body of historical experience became available, these cost items would be admissible for prediction and inclusion in advance programming and decision-making analyses.

5.3 Benefit and Cost Incidence and Matters of Equity

Throughout, it has been emphasized that the incidence of benefits and costs (that is, who receives the benefits and who pays the costs) and the equity or "fairness" of the incidence are issues separate and apart from that of economic efficiency. While some of the important incidence and equity matters were

---

[n]The requirement of actual compensation is, of course, not a necessary condition for determining economic efficiency, but rather is suggested as a means for determining the values involved where no body of experience is presently available.

discussed in subsection 4.3, others deserve attention because of their overall political ramifications and their relationship to the overall decision-making process.

First, in either constant or rising average cost cases, total payments by travelers will be at least as large as the total costs incurred to provide for their tripmaking, while for increasing returns situations, the total payments will be less than the total costs incurred.[o] While society as a whole (that is, in the aggregate) will be better off (in terms of maximizing total net benefits)[p] by carrying out all projects having nonnegative total net benefits, regardless of whether or not total payments at least equal total costs, in the latter case, an income transfer to the travelers (as a group) is implied. Whether or not this subsidy and income transfer is desirable as a social matter depends, of course, on ethical and political judgments and cannot be legitimately debated on strictly technical grounds. While this latter question will not be pursued in depth, it is appropriate to pinpoint at least one aspect bearing on the subject; this involves specification of the characteristics of the group receiving subsidy relative to the general taxpayer, or group from whom the subsidy is received.

While it seems evident that it is not the function of the planner or analyst to resolve these kinds of ethical issues, it is incumbent upon him to detail the consequences of various policy decisions and, more specifically, to describe in detail the circumstances of those affected either adversely or advantageously. It is not necessarily argued that these facts *should* alter the policy decisions, but rather that they *probably will* affect them. One type of information which is useful and important to policy decisions of this sort is knowledge of the income characteristics of those benefiting from, or adversely affected by, the program or project, particularly in those instances where those benefited or disbenefited are a fairly homogeneous group from one end of the income spectrum.

Matters of incidence can assume a particular importance, of course, when parties must pay or endure costs in excess of any benefits or compensation which they may derive. The problem becomes especially acute when non-travelers are burdened with external costs and receive no compensation or less than "adequate" compensation; the situation is even more intense when those disbenefited in this way are members of a low income or minority group. Instances of this sort are receiving increasing amounts of public attention and resistance.

As but three examples of the above, one should consider the circumstances involving the dislocation and disruption accompanying urban highway construction, the noise problems accompanying air transport, and the air pollution stemming from automobile use. For the first two of these, the problem is more clearcut than the third, and generally results from compensating the disadvantaged for less than the amount to which they are disbenefited; while the

---

[o]A single uniform price and short-run marginal cost pricing is assumed.
[p]Again, for all the economic conditions which have been assumed to exist.

conflict may stem partially from a failure to value the external costs properly, it seems reasonable to conclude that it stems more from distributional than economic efficiency matters. (That is, the total net benefits *in the aggregate* probably are positive and the payments probably more than equal the costs *in the aggregate*;[q] thus the conflict stems from distribution of the payments and distribution of the costs, or more simply from lack of concern with the differentials.) Assuming that these two kinds of problems are basically distributional matters, several approaches may be considered. One, what would be the amount necessary to "fairly" compensate the disbenefited for the disruption, dislocation, or noise effects[r] (i.e., the amount necessary to compensate them for the external costs and to avoid their opposition)? Two, what would be the change in total net benefit if the roadway or airport were to be realigned or relocated, such that the external costs were negligible? Three, in the case of the airport, what would be the additional aircraft technology or operating costs required to reduce noise (and perhaps accident) levels to a "negligible" range? Obviously, all of these and other possibilities should be evaluated in order to determine which program or project has the highest (positive) total net benefit; if the best alternative is one that has external costs which, as a political matter, force its rejection *regardless* of whether or not "fair" compensations are made, then the analyst should afford the politician or decision-maker with figures showing the loss in total net benefits stemming from its rejection.

The third example, that of air pollution stemming from automobile usage, is somewhat more complex. If the external costs (to the public at large) were properly included and if the traveler payments were at least to equal the total costs (external costs included), then as a first approximation, one could conclude that there would be no adverse distributional effects. That is, the public would be reimbursed to the extent of the external costs through lowered taxes or, alternatively, public agencies could apply the user payments for the externalities to developing technological devices to reduce toxic elements, and so forth. Of course, another possibility for handling the same problem is to regulate the design and operation of the vehicle's power plant (in terms of toxic elements emitted), as has been done in California, and more recently on a national level.[7] All alternatives—to include both compensation and technological improvement— should be evaluated to determine which one leads to maximization of the total net benefit; should political action force acceptance of less than the most desirable plan, the analyst should detail the extent to which the community's welfare will be reduced.

---

[q]Even if these propositions were not true and if the costs and prices were brought into adjustment, the conflict would remain the same, for all practical purposes. Obviously, the problem is heightened by the impetus afforded by certain political groups and by the press (e.g., consider the San Francisco and Washington, D.C. freeway and the Berkeley highway or subway tussles).

[r]The administrative and practical difficulties of implementing a "fair" compensation policy is of course no mean task, but is ignored here.

The above remarks suggest, of course, that user charges should be differentiated by locale or county, if differences in air pollution and other external costs are to be properly reflected in the user payments. As a general practice, however, this is seldom done, since user taxes and fees are ordinarily imposed uniformly at the state and Federal level; this taxation method by itself will produce income transfers, and will result in undercharging travelers in "critical" counties and overcharging those in noncritical ones (on a relative if not absolute basis). An opposite type of income transfer is implicit, though, in the distribution of the user taxes and fees among the various urban and rural sections of the country, working strongly in favor of the rural areas.[8] On balance, one cannot be certain whether travelers in critical areas do or do not cover the full costs of travel (externalities included). Even so, it seems reasonable to assert that reliance on uniform state and Federal taxes and fees (instead of taxes and fees differentiated locally or by counties) works against proper consideration of externalities, and against development of alternative designs and plans to reduce or eliminate external conditions. (In fact, one can legitimately argue that the present system of state and Federal user taxation works against the investment planning process as a general matter, and operates to overbuild in rural areas and underbuild in urban areas; to some extent, this argument relies on the hypothesis that urban highway transport situations tend to exhibit constant returns to scale, a view that increasingly appears to be valid.)[9]

5.4 Output Units, Nonhomogeneous Costs, and Equilibration

Specification of appropriate output units is of crucial importance to determination of cost, price-volume, and demand functions and to the equilibrating process. The task becomes particularly difficult and complex, as the links being analyzed for possible improvement serve the traveler for only a portion of the entire door-to-door trip, and as the links are utilized by travelers having a wide variety of origin and destination zones.

To illustrate these types of considerations, the region shown in Figure 5-4 and represented by a series of nodes (or origination and termination zones) and by its connecting transport links can be utilized; essentially, we will assume that this set of zones and links is independent of, and isolated from, outside or external effects and activities. To specify the output units, four aspects in particular must be accounted for: (1) the trip unit (i.e., persons, vehicles and their classification, tons, or combination thereof, etc.); (2) the origin and destination of the trip; (3) the links over which the trip is made; and (4) the time interval over which the trips are made, as well as the time-of-day and time period or year during which they are made.

It is necessary to make the above distinctions because the cost and price-volume functions will vary from link to link, and with changes in the trip

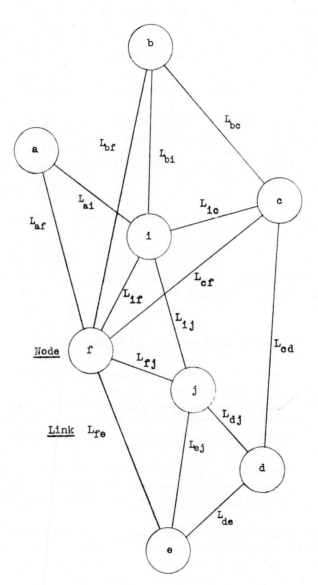

Figure 5-4. Isolated Link and Node Travel System.

unit and time interval, and demand will vary for different origin and destination node pairs, times of day, and time periods, as well as for other factors. Equilibration will therefore require that the cost, price-volume, and demand functions are internally consistent, and stated in terms of equivalent output measures accounting for these four aspects. Equilbration will also be complicated in two other major respects ignored thus far. One, the demand for travel between any two nodes or zones i and j is not just dependent upon the equilibrium travel circumstances or travel price for link L_{ij}, but also upon the equilibrium travel prices for other routes connecting nodes i and j (such as L_{if} + L_{fj} or L_{ic} + L_{cd} + L_{dj}). Two, the equilibrium quantity demanded and travel price on each of the links connecting nodes i and j (including L_{ij}), is dependent not just upon the demand for travel between nodes i and j, but is dependent on the travel demand between other pairs of nodes which can be made over the same links; for instance, the equilibrium flow on link L_{ij} can consist of trips being made between a and j, between a and d, between c and j, and so forth. For other than those circumstances where a link, and the demand for travel over that link, can be isolated from all other portions of the network or system, a situation which is rare, and compares to that for the equilibrium models formulated in earlier chapters and sections, it will be necessary to use iterative computational procedures for determining the equilibrium flow and price conditions (regardless of the pricing policy). These iterative procedures will have to simultaneously take account of the demand functions for all pairs of nodes, and of the cost functions for each of the links, all as they relate to each other.[10]

In making equilibrations of the sort outlined above, proper specification of the output unit is of key importance because of its relationship to demand, cost, and price-volume functions. Thus far, all these functions were presumed to have output units of vehicle trips *per hour*;[11] furthermore, the output was assumed to include only passenger trips, each vehicle trip was assumed to be identical in terms of the number of passengers per vehicle, and all travelers were assumed to perceive identical private travel costs (for travel time, effort, tolls, and vehicle ownership and operation).

To correctly handle these aspects (as well as intratemporal and intermodal demand cross-elasticities) will not change the principles of the investment planning and benefit-cost analysis, but will markedly increase the difficulties and complexities of the equilibration procedure and probably will alter significantly the final outcomes (i.e., the design choice and staging plan). The data requirements will also be *enormously* increased by replacement of the above assumptions with more suitable representations. In the following paragraphs, some guidelines for integrating these more practical considerations will be outlined; clearly, though, their specific form and detail will depend on the outcome of more intensive data analyses.

First, it is evident that the cost price-volume functions should not be restricted to output stated simply in terms of passenger tripmaking; that is, congestion and travel time on specific links of a highway transport system—such as that shown schematically in Figure 5-4—depend both on cargo and passenger tripmaking, and thus on tripmaking in trucks, buses and passenger vehicles. As a consequence, it will be necessary to jointly consider the demand for cargo movement and that for passenger movement, and to carry out equilibration while considering the interaction of cargo and passenger vehicles, which use and congest the same facilities and links; in simple terms, this will require that demand be stratified or dimensioned by type of movement (or, say, by vehicle type—heavy truck, light truck, bus, taxi, and both single and multiple passenger car). Furthermore, since these different types of movement will be made over the same facilities or links, the cost and price-volume functions for each movement type will be dependent on the joint output, whose units must therefore be expressed in terms of all types of vehicle units; in essence, this means that it will be necessary to determine cost and price-volume relationships for *each* type of movement as a function of the *total* movement volume, and the proportion of trips made by each type. The equilibration procedure to account for these interdependencies will necessarily be most complex, particularly if the intermodal and intramodal demand cross-elasticities are also to be handled. (Clearly, the cross-elasticities should be characterized and integrated, since passenger shifts among bus, taxi, and auto (drive alone and car pool) modes will occur in practice, as will both passenger and cargo shifts, from hour to hour during the day.)

Second, it is important to characterize the differences among individual travelers with respect to the way in which they perceive and evaluate certain travel costs, and with respect to auto purchases, car pooling, and other significant preferences and tradeoffs. Without question, there are wide variations in the manner and extent to which travelers consider, and are affected by, travel time and congestion, vehicle ownership and accident payments, and the inconvenience of car pooling.[12] While it is clear that travelers whose trip value (i.e., the value of making a specific trip to some particular destination) is high will be willing to endure higher private travel prices in order to make the trip than will those with lower trip values, it cannot be assumed that those with higher trip values will necessarily regard the private inconvenience or discomfort of car pooling or of congestion as being more "costly" than will those travelers having low trip values. Thus, since the output consists of travelers having different trip values, and having different travel service preferences with respect to auto quality, parking convenience, car pooling, and traffic congestion, and since trip values and travel service preferences are only partly dependent on income level, equilibration cannot (necessarily) be accomplished accurately by simply stratifying demand and price-volume functions by income level. However, one might attempt to equilibrate demand and price-volume functions stratified by income level as a first approximation for more accurate estimates (which, say, are to be determined by iterative procedures).

It appears that satisfactory treatment of these variations in travel price, which are dependent both on the level of output and on the particular groups of people and goods involved in tripmaking, will require highly complex simulation models to accomplish equilibration; and it would appear that iterative trial-and-error procedures offer the only hope for simultaneously satisfying the intricate demand and price-volume conditions. However, even these kinds of procedures may lead to multiple solutions and ambiguities. Considerable research and investigation must be undertaken before any firm conclusions can be reached on their dimensions, reliability, or accuracy.

However, once simulation models can be constructed, so as to more realistically depict the actual demand and price-volume conditions (cross-elasticities included), and to determine the actual equilibrium flow and travel prices resulting therefrom, the benefit-cost analysis framework and procedures outlined earlier in Chapter 4 will be applicable. Thus, the major difficulty rests with the problems of gathering and processing the data requisite to the formulation of multidimensioned and compatible demand, cost, and price-volume functions, and with the enormous intellectual and electronic data processing resources necessary to simulate the realistic conditions for regions and networks.

Summary, Conclusions, and Statement of Research Needs

Investment planning for public facilities has been explored in a two-step sequence. First, the overall driver-vehicle-roadway system components and variables which affect investment decisions were defined, and their relationships to one another and to the planning process were outlined for static economic conditions. In this way, an attempt was made to explain in approximate terms the interworkings of investment planning, the effects of changes in facility design or control, and the effects of shifts in demand. Second, the analysis and evaluation procedures necessary to determine the consequences, and judge the worthwhileness of different facility designs, control or pricing schemes, or staging plans were outlined; these models were intended to permit evaluation in terms of their overall economic effects to the public, and in terms of their financial feasibility, while accounting for dynamic changes in prices, opportunity costs, discount rates, demand, and facility designs.

More specifically, the nature and description of transport were delineated from the public point of view; then the relationships of costs and cost functions to the facility size (or capacity level), to the facility usage (or output level), and to the time dimension was spelled out. Also, the differences between market values and opportunity costs, and the importance of external costs to the analysis were discussed, and the aspects important to specifying "an appropriate" discount rate were summarized.

The general nature of demand functions and of intratemporal and intertemporal changes was outlined, as well as their use in determining travel benefits. Of key importance, the interaction between demand and price-volume functions (for different pricing policies and flow control devices), and use of these functions for equilibration and travel forecasting, were treated in detail. Also, the difficulties of specifying demand functions from empirical data were described, and an illustrative problem provided insight into the mechanics of equilibration procedures.

The cost, price-volume, and demand functions serve as the essential determinants of equilibrium flow and price conditions, and in turn of the economic efficiency and financial feasibility of projects; these aspects were described in Chapter 4, along with their relationship to facility expansion, to the pricing policy, and to the time of occurrence (of expansion and usage). Once the dynamic nature of investment planning is accounted for, and after consideration of both intertemporal and intratemporal demand fluctuations, it becomes necessary to analyze and evaluate different facility plans and their staging sequences, as well as different pricing policies, by making use of benefit-cost procedures. Specifically, the analyst should make use of net present value (or present worth) techniques to analyze the incremental effects of facility improvement or operation, and to discount benefits and costs occurring during different time periods to a comparable time base. The discounting and analysis techniques were outlined to permit evaluation of economic efficiency and financial returns of projects under various staging plans; also in Chapter 4, the pricing and equilibrium conditions leading to optimal efficiency for facilities were spelled out. However, these equilibrium conditions applied only for the strict assumptions set forth (regarding equal and constant marginal utility of income, marginal cost pricing throughout the economy, and so forth).

Finally, in Chapter 5 it was necessary to introduce some of the more practical considerations which add to the difficulty and complexity of investment planning, and to consider how the planning process might generally be affected. First, the consequences and costs of implementing different sorts of pricing policies were examined, and the benefit-cost analysis procedures were modified to permit evaluation of the economic effects of the alternative pricing policies. From this discussion, it was concluded that no *a priori* or general statements could be made regarding the "best" or most economically efficient pricing policy in any particular investment situation; rather, judgments on such matters depend on a detailed examination of the changes in equilibrium flow, price, benefits, and costs stemming from each alternative—as well as on ethical judgments regarding the "equitability" of the alternatives. Second, attention was devoted to the problems raised by the measurement of externalities and consumer surpluses, and to the inconsistencies between public and private investment planning analyses which sometimes occur. Some possibilities for characterizing these costs and benefit circumstances were outlined. Third, some discussion dealt with the modifications required in order to account for joint usage of facilities by passenger and goods vehicles, and for variations in vehicle occupancy and private perceived travel expenditures. Also, attention was devoted to the procedures for equilibrating demand and price-volume conditions as they are affected by network characteristics, and by tripmaking over links which consist of people and goods having different pairs of origin and destination points. These more realistic network effects will complicate trip forecasting or equilibration procedures significantly, and will add greatly to the data needs and data processing requirements, even to calculate the equilibrium flows and travels during just one demand period (say, that for the peak period) for only one time period or year. However, it is important to emphasize that a realistic analysis should account not only for the travel and price conditions during, say, the peak period or peak hour of the so-called "design year," but also for those during both peak and off-peak periods, and for all years during the planning horizon (or "foreseeable" future).

The investment planning framework which has been presented differs considerably from that usually taught and practiced by highway and transit planners; these differences warrant a brief summarization in order to clarify and pinpoint those areas of research which need most attention. First, costs and benefits have been described in terms of effects on the public welfare and on the traveler; the distinction is necessary to properly measure economic efficiency of public investments, to realistically forecast actual tripmaking (or equilibrium flow), and to relate these two important aspects. Also, costs and benefits have been described in terms of the time frame (i.e., short-run or long-run and time period or year of occurrence), and in terms of their relationship to output level, facility size, and pricing policy (or other control devices); these distinctions—while commonly neglected by engineers and planners—are requisite to accurate forecasting, to appropriate treatment of the time value of resources, to determination of both economic and financial feasibility, and to proper analysis of the incremental and overall economic and financial conditions. They are of particular importance to the evaluation of different staging or sequencing plans for various projects. While some research on highway transport costing has been conducted in these terms, though mostly by transportation economists outside of the highway engineering and planning community, it is reasonable to suggest that far too little has been undertaken, and that these aspects deserve considerably more attention and research before they can be suitably documented.

Second, the extremely important subjects of demand, travel forecasting, and benefit measurement have been described in terms far different from those familiar to highway and transit engineers and planners. These differences, far from being mere definitional matters, deserve more than scant attention. Essentially, travel forecasting and benefit measurement have been cast in terms of travelers, in terms of the performance characteristics of the physical system and vehicles serving the tripmaking function, and in terms of the hour-to-hour, day-to-day, and year-to-year shifts in the economy and environment as they are related to tripmaking; more importantly, these aspects have been related as they affect tripmaking, benefit measurement, and economic efficiency. In simpler terms, the travel forecasting task (or say, UTP process) *usually* is depicted as one of distributing a *fixed* number of trips generated by zone *i* among all other attraction zones (in which the number of trips attracted to zone *j* is *fixed*), of splitting the interzonal transfers between transit and auto modes, and of assigning the modal interzonal transfers among the different modal routes; such a forecasting technique, as a practical matter, assumes that demand (at the origination and attraction zones) is perfectly inelastic with respect to equilibrium flow and travel prices, and is illogical conceptually, since it is implicitly assumed that tripmaking is not dependent on the facility design or other important system factors. Herein, though, trip generation as well as modal split and route assignment is made dependent on the facility design and the resultant travel conditions. While taking these interdependencies into account will require some considerable data gathering and analysis and research (say, of the sort outlined in Appendix 2 and carried out in the early phases of the Boston-Washington Corridor study), such comprehensive demand models do offer a high expectation of improving our forecasting capabilities.

Third, procedures have been described for analyzing and evaluating the economic consequences of different sorts of pricing and control devices, as well as those of different facility sizes and staging plans. These procedures—rather than presenting the engineering design and investment planning problem as one of designing facilities to meet arbitrary design standards and of evaluating the average variable costs during only *one* arbitrarily chosen "design year"—have been outlined to permit examination of the dynamic hour-to-hour and year-to-year travel costs and benefits, over the entire n year planning horizon; furthermore, the suggested types of dynamic and incremental benefit-cost analyses will permit the engineer to properly reflect changes in factor prices, discount rates, incomes, and technology, over time, and to regard the staging of improvements to the transport system, or even its abandonment, as design variables. The success of these more comprehensive analyses depends on the quality of the research directed at better forecasts for the uncertain future, and on proper treatment of the aspects of risk and uncertainty.

Finally, if there can be any finding or conclusion of real meaning, it would be that there is no clearcut rule or policy for investment planning or pricing which *assures* that public welfare is maximized. Rather, it is first necessary to propose, to analyze and evaluate the consequences of the virtual infinity of possible technological, staging, and pricing alternatives—in the face of, and accounting for, the uncertain future; next, it is necessary to detail the incremental costs or loss in total net benefit which results from adopting political or ethical criteria that conflict with more singular economic welfare criteria, and to afford the policy-makers with this information. To undertake (much less accomplish) such a task will require enormous intellectual resources, not to speak of the requisite analytical and data resources. However, if one is to even approach the task of system planning and to make conclusions about "better" or "best" plans, other than by chance, these commitments will probably be necessary. Whether undertaking the effort and committing the resources necessary to accomplish an "adequate" planning job is justifiable, is a judgment I leave to the reader, to the academician, and to those supporting the labors of the researcher.

Appendixes

Appendix 1: Relationships Among Demand, Price Elasticity, Marginal Revenue, and Total Revenue

Demand should be viewed as a statement of people's tripmaking propensities; that is, it should be viewed as a demand *function* or *conditional* tripmaking relationship. Thus, a demand function represents the dependence of the quantity of tripmaking to be demanded upon the price of tripmaking.

For the initial remarks, restrict your attention to, say, a specific transit service (operation with some known, fixed schedule, etc.), the demand for which can be represented as shown in Figure A1-1. Generally, and as shown in Figure A1-1, a price drop (such as from p_1 to p_2) will increase the quantity of trips demanded during that time period; for this case, the increase in tripmaking induced by the price reduction was Δq.

To determine the degree of change in tripmaking which takes place as a result of price changes, the analyst makes use of a central characteristic or descriptor of demand functions called "elasticity." For example, the "elasticity of demand with respect to price" is a dimensionless measure of the degree to which travelers respond to price changes.

Specifically, the elasticity (e_p or η_p) is defined as follows:

$$e_p \text{ or } \eta_p = \% \text{ change in quantity demanded which accompanies a 1\% change in price}$$

$$= \frac{\text{relative change in quantity}}{\text{relative change in price}}$$

$$= \frac{\partial q/q}{\partial p/p} \text{ or, better, } \frac{\Delta q/q}{\Delta p/p} \quad . \tag{A1-1}$$

The portion of the demand function which has an elasticity value which is less than (i.e., more negative than) -1 is termed the elastic region, while that portion having an elasticity value between 0 and -1 is the inelastic portion. The elasticities for two forms of (single-variable) demand functions are shown on Figure A1-2. Note that for a linear demand model the elasticity varies over its entire range, while for a nonlinear model of the hyperbolic (or so-called "log/log") form, the elasticity is constant.

Equation (A1-1) can be used to determine the elasticity at some point along the demand function. For the linear form, it can be shown that:

$$e_p = 1 - \beta/q \quad . \tag{A1-2}$$

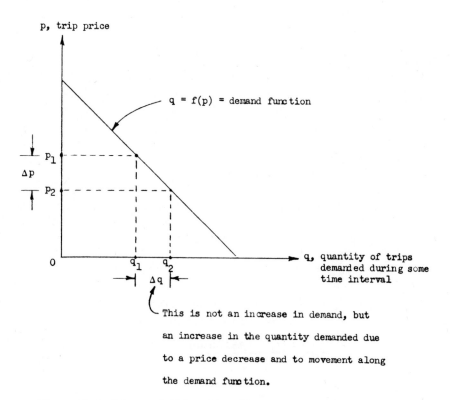

Note: The dependent and independent variable axes have been reversed (to follow the usual convention).

p, trip price

q = f(p) = demand function

p_1

Δp

p_2

0

q_1 q_2

Δq

q, quantity of trips demanded during some time interval

This is not an increase in demand, but an increase in the quantity demanded due to a price decrease and to movement along the demand function.

Figure A1-1. Price and Tripmaking Changes for a Linear Demand Function.

However, to determine the elasticity accompanying more than a slight price change, then the following formula should be used:

$$e_p = \frac{\Delta q / \overline{q}}{\Delta p / \overline{p}} \; . \qquad (A1\text{-}3)$$

where Δq is the change in tripmaking which results from a price change of Δp, $\overline{q}$ is the average of the before and after tripmaking quantities, and $\overline{p}$ is the average of the before and after trip prices.

One of the questions of special interest to the transit or toll road operator (to name but two interested parties) is: How will the total (or gross) and net revenues change as a result of price changes? For this purpose, the elasticity measure permits determination of the changes in revenues and volume and, in turn, the changes in road capacity, toll booths, or rolling stock, which stem from altering the toll or fare structure. For a transit or toll operator, for example, changes in the number of buses needed and gross revenues can be calculated. The practical usefulness of knowledge about elasticities, while virtually unutilized in urban transport circles, cannot be overstated. For example, if transit fares are currently within the elastic portion of the demand curve, a decrease in price *without a change in service or schedule frequency* will increase ridership and gross revenues. (An increase in net revenues may or may not result, depending on the increase in costs stemming from the extra ridership.) On the other hand, if fares are presently within the inelastic region of the demand function, an increase in fare *without changing service or schedule frequency* will decrease ridership and costs, while increasing the gross *and* net revenues. Similarly, the utility of such knowledge (that is, is the demand elastic or inelastic and to what extent?) to toll road and transit authorities, railroads, airlines, etc., is all too obvious. Clearly, though, this knowledge can only fully be exploited by also having information on the accompanying cost changes.

To be specific about the details of the above remarks, let us deal analytically with these aspects for the *linear* demand function shown in Figure A1-2(a), and for a price change such as indicated in Figure A1-1.

First, $TR(q)$, the total revenues for a *uniform* price of p and a resultant tripmaking volume of q, would be:

$$TR(q) = p \cdot q = (\beta/\alpha - q/\alpha)q$$
$$= \beta q/\alpha - q^2/\alpha \quad . \tag{A1-4}$$

Then, let *marginal* revenue or $mr(q)$ be defined as the change in total revenue which occurs when the tripmaking quantity q increases by *one* unit.[a] Then, for the linear demand function in which

$$q = \beta - \alpha p \tag{A1-5}$$

and, inversely, in which

$$p = \beta/\alpha - q/\alpha \quad , \tag{A1-6}$$

the marginal revenue function would be as follows:

$$mr(q) = \frac{\Delta TR(q)}{\Delta q}$$

---

[a]Obviously, tripmaking can be increased only by a slight decrease in price.

$$= \frac{\partial TR(q)}{\partial q}$$

$$= \beta/\alpha - 2q/\alpha \quad . \tag{A1-7}$$

Note that the marginal revenue function has a slope which is twice that of the inverse demand or price function shown by equation (A1-6), *and* that the marginal revenue is zero when the quantity demanded is $\beta/2$, or at the volume level corresponding to the unit elastic point. See Figures A1-2(a) and A1-3. The meaning is straightforward: (1) to increase tripmaking above $\beta/2$ (which can only be accomplished by reducing the price) will reduce total revenues and,

(a) Linear Demand Function

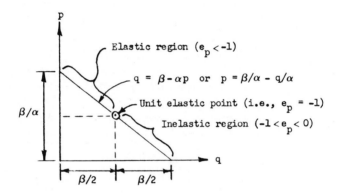

(b) Non-Linear Demand Function (Hyperbolic Form)

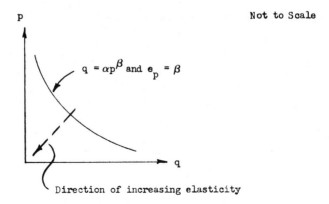

Figure A1-2. Single Variable Linear and Nonlinear Demand Functions.

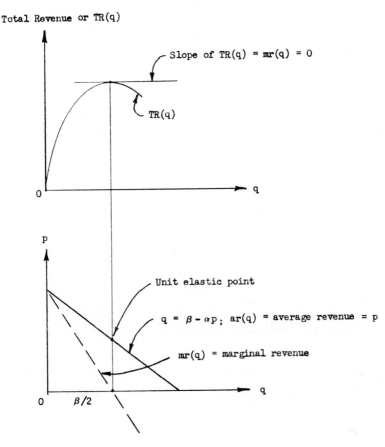

Figure A1-3. Total Revenue, Average Revenue, and Marginal Revenue Functions for a Linear Demand Curve.

similarly, to reduce tripmaking below $\beta/2$ (by increasing prices) will reduce total revenues; and (2) total revenues are at a maximum when the price is at the unit elastic point (i.e., when $e_p = -1$). (These points are illustrated in Figure A1-3.) Thus, no revenues are gained or lost by *small* price changes at the unit elastic point. However, in the *elastic* region, price *decreases* can increase the gross revenues.

Finally, it should be pointed out that price increases in the *inelastic* region of the demand function will increase *both* the total *and* net revenues for the facility or system (since tripmaking and thus costs are simultaneously being reduced). Contrarily, no such statement about net revenue increases can be made for price reductions in the elastic region, since the cost increases accompanying the ridership increases may or may not exceed the total revenue increases. In any case, the significance of knowing the elasticities in the region of the present fare or price level, and more especially in that for which price changes are contemplated, is obvious.

Appendix 2: Demand Functions to Account for Intratemporal and Intermodal Relations and Cross Relations: A First Approximation

The amount of tripmaking (between any two zones, i and j) at time t by mode m is not only dependent on the price (or, say, travel time and fare or toll) for travel by mode m at time t, but also depends on the other travel opportunities that will be available; that is, it also depends on the travel price on each of the other modes at time t, and it depends on the travel prices at all other times of day for each of the modes (mode m included).

For describing these relationships between tripmaking and travel prices, use will be made of the demand elasticities and cross-elasticities for all modal and temporal (or time-of-day) possibilities. The demand elasticity for travel by mode m at time t, with respect to the travel price, is the percentage change in travel by mode m at time t which results from a one-percent increase in the travel price by mode m at time t; the intratemporal demand cross-elasticity for travel by mode m at time t, with respect to travel by mode m at time y, is the percentage change in travel by mode m at time t which results from a one-percent increase in the travel price by mode m at time y. Similarly, the intermodal demand cross-elasticity for travel time by mode m at time t, with respect to travel by mode x at time t, is the percentage change in travel by mode m, which results from a one-percent increase in the travel price by mode x at time t. Finally, the intratemporal and intermodal demand cross-elasticity for travel by mode m at time t, with respect to travel by mode x at time y, is the percentage change in travel by mode m at time t which results from a one-percent increase in the travel price by mode x at time y.

While the specific details and form of the demand function would depend on the outcome of a comprehensive data analysis (involving both cross-sectional and time-series data), the general structure might be hypothesized to be of the following exponential form:

$$D_{ij}^{m,t} = \alpha_m Y_i^{\beta_m} P_i^{\gamma_m} E_j^{\delta_m} \prod_{x,y} (c_{ij}^{x,y})^{\theta_{m,t,x,y}} \prod_{x,y} (f_{ij}^{x,y})^{\phi_{m,t,x,y}} \quad \text{(A2-1)}$$

where

$D_{ij}^{m,t}$ = Number of trips (or quantity of trips demanded) between zones i and j by mode m at time t.

$c_{ij}^{x,y}$ = Travel time or congestion measure (in minutes, say) for trips between zones i and j by mode x at time y.

135

$f^{x,y}_{ij}$ = Travel fare or toll for trips between zones i and j by mode x at time y.

Y_i = Median household income for residents of zone i.

P_i = Population in zone i.

E_j = Employment in zone j.

α_m = Parameter for travel by mode m.

β_m = % change in travel by mode m at time t resulting from 1% change in zone i income.

γ_m = % change in travel by mode m at time t resulting from 1% change in zone i population.

δ_m = % change in travel by mode m at time t resulting from 1% change in zone j employment.

$\theta_{m,t,x,y}$ = % change in travel by mode m at time t resulting from 1% change in travel time by mode x at time y.

$\phi_{m,t,x,y}$ = % change in travel by mode m at time t resulting from 1% change in travel fare by mode x at time y.

In equation (A2-1) the exponents β_m, γ_m, δ_m are the demand elasticities for travel by mode m at time t with respect to income, population, and employment, respectively; $\theta_{m,t,x,y}$ (or $\phi_{m,t,x,y}$) is the demand cross-elasticity for travel by mode m at time t with respect to the travel time (or travel fare) by mode x at time y.

If the logarithm is taken of both sides of equation (A2-1), the resultant equation may be regarded as a multiple linear regression, and the coefficients of this log form of the demand function may be determined by the method of least squares.[a]

The input data necessary to determine the elasticities for such a demand model would be:

1. Interzonal trip movements for all (or as many as possible) pairs of zones, by mode and time of day; that is $D^{x,y}_{ij}$ for all i, j, x and y;
2. Median household incomes by residence zone; that is, Y_i for all i;
3. Population by residence zone; that is, P_i for all i;
4. Employment by employment zone; that is, E_j for all j;
5. Measures of travel time and congestion (say, in minutes) for all pairs of zones, by mode and time of day; that is, $c^{x,y}_{ij}$ for all $i, j, x,$ and y; and
6. Tolls or fares for trips between all pairs of zones, by mode and time of day; that is, $f^{x,y}_{ij}$ for all $i, j, x,$ and y.

---

[a]Such a model would, of course, embody certain assumptions about normality, equal variances, constant elasticities, etc., all of which should be subjected to additional analysis.

The demand function as formulated in equation (A2-1) implies that the elasticities and cross-elasticities remain *constant* for all ranges of travel congestion and fare, for all income levels, etc., an assumption of doubtful validity at best. To test such an assumption (to the extent possible), cross-sectional data of the sort outlined in the six steps above should be analyzed for different time periods and for a *range* of travel prices, incomes, and so forth (preferably to include the conditions for which the model is to be used as predictive device). Where time-series (or other) data indicate that the elasticities or cross-elasticities are not constant, and this appears to be the case,[1] the demand model can be modified in a number of ways. In the simplest case, the exponents of the independent variables (or elasticities and cross-elasticities) can be expressed as linear functions of time, say, and estimated (as before) by least squares, multiple regression analysis. However, for nonlinear exponents or more complicated interdependencies, much more sophisticated analysis is required to estimate the elasticities.

· For a detailed description of a situation in which this type of formulation and statistical procedure was used for determining the various elasticities, see the report on the intercity passenger demand model developed by Gerald Kraft for the Systems Analysis and Research Corporation for use in the Boston-Washington corridor.[2] For a more recent analysis and development of this *general* type of demand model (through one applying to urban transport modes), see: "An Evaluation of Free Transit Service," Report by Charles River Associates to Office of Economics, Department of Transportation, Washington, D.C., August 1968.

Appendix 3: Linear Programming Formulation for Nonlinear Toll Pricing Model

Maximize $z = 3q_1 + 2q_2 + 9q_3 + 10q_4$, subject to nonnegativity restrictions and the following constraints:[a]

$$q_1 + 35.8p = 11,000$$
$$q_2 + 36.6p = 10,000 \quad \text{Demand Function}$$
$$q_3 + 31.0p = 8,000 \quad \text{Constraints}$$
$$q_4 + 32.0p = 4,600$$

$$p_i - 0.14q - t \geqslant -1352$$
$$p_i - 0.05q - t \geqslant -362$$
$$p_i - 0.024\,q - t \geqslant -102 \quad \text{User Price-Volume}$$
$$p_i - 0.011q - t \geqslant 8.5 \quad\quad \text{Constraints}$$
$$p_i - 0.00534q - t \geqslant 45.5$$
$$p_i - 0.00286q - t \geqslant 54$$

$$t + 0.008625(3q_1 + 2q_2 + 9q_3 + 10q_4) \geqslant 103.45$$
$$t + 0.000860(3q_1 + 2q_2 + 9q_3 + 10q_4) \geqslant 25.8 \quad \text{Roadway}$$
$$t + 0.000285(3q_1 + 2q_2 + 9q_3 + 10q_4) \geqslant 24.30 \quad \text{Toll}$$
$$t + 0.000115(3q_1 + 2q_2 + 9q_3 + 10q_4) \geqslant 9.20 \quad \text{Con-}$$
$$t + 0.000023(3q_1 + 2q_2 + 9q_3 + 10q_4) \geqslant 4.60 \quad \text{straints}$$
$$t \geqslant 1.15$$

---

[a]Coefficients from Figures 3-8, 3-9, and 3-10. Also, for a more complete formulation dealing with demand cross-elasticities as well, see: Wohl, 1970.

Row No.	OBJ1	Q1	Q2	Q3	Q4	P1	P2	P3	P4	T	B1
1	-1	-3	-2	-9	-10						0
2		1				35.8					11,000
3			1				36.6				10,000
4				1				31.0			8,000
5					1				32.0		4,600
6		-0.14				1				-1	-1,352
7			-0.14				1			-1	-1,352
8				-0.14				1		-1	-1,352
9					-0.14				1	-1	-1,352
10		-0.05				1				-1	-362
11			-0.05				1			-1	-362
12				-0.05				1		-1	-362
13					-0.05				1	-1	-362
14		-0.024				1				-1	-102
15			-0.024				1			-1	-102
16				-0.024				1		-1	-102
17					-0.024				1	-1	-102
18		-0.011				1				-1	8.5
19			-0.011				1			-1	8.5
20				-0.011				1		-1	8.5
21					-0.011				1	-1	8.5
22		-0.0053				1				-1	45.5
23			-0.0053				1			-1	45.5
24				-0.0053				1		-1	45.5
25					-0.0053				1	-1	45.5

141

Row No.	OBJ1	Q1	Q2	Q3	Q4	P1	P2	P3	P4	T	B1
26		−0.0029				1				−1	54
27			−0.0029				1			−1	54
28				−0.0029				1		−1	54
29					−0.0029				1	−1	54
30		0.025875	0.017250	0.077625	0.086250					1	103.45
31		0.00258	0.00172	0.007740	0.00860					1	25.8
32		0.000855	0.000570	0.002565	0.002850					1	14.3
33		0.000345	0.000230	0.001035	0.001150					1	9.2
34		0.000069	0.000046	0.000207	0.000230					1	4.6
35										1	1.15

Notes

Notes

Chapter 1
The Transportation Investment Problem

1. More will be said about this point later. Also, this practice appears to be reasonably common among transportation economists. See, for instance: M. Beckmann, et al., *Studies in the Economics of Transportation* (New Haven, Conn.: Yale University Press, 1956), pp. 48 ff.; L. Wingo, *Transportation and Urban Land* (Resources for the Future, Inc., 1954), pp. 52 ff.; A.A. Walters, *The Economics of Road User Charges* (International Bank for Reconstruction and Development, 1968), chaps. 2 and 3; and W. Vickrey, "Pricing as a Tool in Coordination of Local Transportation," *Transportation Economics*, National Bureau of Economic Research, Columbia University Press, 1965.

2. J. Hirshleifer, J.C. DeHaven, and J.W. Milliman, *Water Supply: Economics, Technology, and Policy* (Chicago: The University of Chicago Press, 1960), p. 36.

3. This type of analysis dates from the nineteenth century. E.L. Grant's writings represent the most complete modern-day expression, particularly: E.L. Grant and W.G. Ireson, *Principles of Engineering Economy* (New York: The Ronald Press, 1960).

4. Essentially the same assumption is virtually always made, implicitly if not explicitly. For the latter, see: Beckmann, et al., *Transportation*, p. 51 and A.A. Walters, "The Theory and Measurement of Private and Social Cost of Highway Congestion," *Econometrica,* **29**, 4 (October 1961), p. 677.

5. See for example Beckmann et al., *Transportation*, chap. 2.

6. Walters, *Econometrica*, p. 677.

7. Grant and Ireson, *Engineering Economy*, pp. 445-56.

8. T.E. Kuhn, *Public Enterprise Economics and Transport Problems* (California: University of California Press, 1962), p. 13. Earlier, on p. 8, Kuhn noted, definitionally, that "external values can be defined as signals not received by the decision maker but by other parties, and internal values as effects that are of definite concern to him."

9. Ibid., Table 2 and pp. 55-66.

10. R. Zettel, "Highway Benefit and Cost Analysis as an Aid to Investment Decision," Reprint No. 49, Institute of Transportation and Traffic Engineering, University of California.

11. By contrast, the Doyle Report emphatically concluded that, "In consonance with the basic objective of Federal policy, governmental actions at *all* levels should be taken in the national public interest. Conflicting interest must, of necessity, yield to the greater good of all." [emphasis added] (from *National Transportation Policy*, Report for U.S. Senate Committee on Interstate and

Foreign Commerce, U.S. Government Printing Office, Washington, D.C., January 1961).

Chapter 2
Transport Cost Functions

1. Two good references which provide more details for this subject are: A. Maass et al., *Design of Water Resource Systems* (Cambridge: Harvard University Press, 1962), chapter 3 by R. Dorfman and R. Dorfman, *The Price System* (New Jersey: Prentice-Hall, 1964), chap. 2.

2. Obviously there is a continuum between the short- and long-run as defined here. For a more elaborate treatment dealing with this point, see: M. Friedman, *Price Theory: A Provisional Text* (Chicago: Aldine Publishing Company, 1962), pp. 111 ff.

3. For a good discussion of this point, see Maass et al., *Water Resource*, pp. 49 ff and pp. 198 ff. Also, the opportunity costs of inputs may be defined as the revenues from other alternative investments which must be foregone in order to acquire the inputs.

4. Such a construct is somewhat different than that normally employed by many economists, but is consistent with the formulation often adopted by economists in dealing with transport matters. See, for example: M. Beckmann et al., *Studies in the Economics of Transportation* (New Haven, Conn.: Yale University Press, 1956), chaps. 2 and 4; W. Vickrey, "Pricing as a Tool in Coordination of Local Transportation," *Transportation Economics*, National Bureau of Economic Research, Columbia University Press, 1965; and A.A. Walters, *The Economics of Road User Charges* (International Bank for Reconstruction and Development, 1968), chaps. 2 and 3.

5. Substantially the same assumption has been made by A.A. Walters, M. Beckmann, W. Vickrey and others, as noted previously.

6. The discussion on this subject area is lengthy; some of the better references are: R.N. McKean, *Efficiency in Government Through Systems Analysis* (New York: Wiley, 1964), chap. 8; J. Margolis, "Secondary Benefits, External Economies, and the Justification of Public Investment," *Review of Economics and Statistics,* **39** (1957), p. 284.

7. Margolis, in commenting on a number of important studies which dealt (in part) with this problem, said, ". . . general procedures by which to discover the technological external economies are absent . . . Unfortunately, the necessary studies of economies of scale in areas where these projects are being located are not far enough advanced to permit the analyst to make reasonable estimates of the economies of scale." J. Margolis, "The Economic Evaluation of Federal Water Resource Development," (a review article), *The American Economic Review,* **49**, 1 (March 1959), p. 108.

8. For a good discussion of this point see: J. Hirshleifer, J.C. DeHaven, and J.W. Milliman, *Water Supply: Economics, Technology, and Policy* (Chicago: The University of Chicago Press, 1960), p. 128.

9. For a discussion of this point, see: Maass et al., *Water Resource*, pp. 49 ff. and Hirshleifer, DeHaven, and Milliman, *Water Supply*, pp. 77 ff. Also, this remark on the differential between market prices and true costs applies to all cost items, not just fixed costs.

10. Winfrey, among others, makes this same point in some pertinent examples; see: R. Winfrey, "Concepts and Applications of Engineering Economy in the Highway Field," *Highway Research Board Special Report* 56, Washington, D.C., 1959, pp. 24 ff.

11. See: G.P. St. Clair and N. Lieder, "Evaluation of Unit Cost of Time and Strain-and-Discomfort Cost of Non-Uniform Driving," *Highway Research Board Special Report* 56, Washington, D.C., pp. 116 ff.; also, M. Wohl, "The Short-Run Congestion Cost and Pricing Dilemma," *Traffic Quarterly* (January 1966), pp. 54-59, hereinafter cited Wohl, 1966.

12. The literature dealing with the specific cost items is lengthy; a useful bibliography is included in *Highway Research Board Special Report* 56, pp. 180 ff. Useful references for costing methodology are: J.R. Meyer et al., *The Economics of Competitition in the Transportation Industries* (Cambridge: Harvard University Press, 1959), chaps. 2 through 5; J. Meyer et al., *The Urban Transportation Problem* (Cambridge: Harvard University Press, 1965), chaps. 8-11.

13. For further discussion of this point, see: M. Wohl, "Determination of Peak and Off-Peak Costs, Prices and Demands Under Certain Pricing Conditions and Facility Cost Allocation Methods," Discussion Paper No. 26, *Harvard Transport Research Program* (August 1965).

14. For a derivation and full discussion of this cost function, see: Wohl, 1966. Also, the accuracy of this particular formulation is not argued herein; rather, I use it to illustrate the mechanics of cost functions and of their interaction with demand functions.

15. In Maass et al., *Water Resource*, pp. 194 ff. See also remarks on pp. 47 ff.

16. An excellent discussion of these aspects may be found in "Standards and Criteria for Formulating and Evaluating Federal Water Resources Developments," *Report to Bureau of the Budget* by M. Hufschmidt, J. Krutilla and Julius Margolis (with assistance of S.A. Marglin), Washington, D.C. (June 1961), pp. 11 ff.

17. Arguments with respect to these two points are made forcefully by Hirshleifer, DeHaven, and Milliman, *Water Supply*, pp. 116 ff. The entire matter of discounting and of the discount rate is summarized carefully and concisely in Chaps. 6 and 7, material which is well worth reading.

18. Margolis, *Federal Water*, pp. 102-03.

19. This rate was estimated prior to 1958 and would probably be higher

today. For Eckstein's discussion on interest rate selection, see: O. Eckstein, *Water-Resource Development* (Cambridge: Harvard University Press, 1958), chap. 4, sec. 3.

20. Hufschmidt et al., *Criteria*, p. 15.

21. Ibid., p. 15.

22. This subject will only be treated in brief terms; also, little distinction will be made between "risk" and "uncertainty." For a thorough and straightforward treatment of investment planning under uncertainty, see: H. Bierman, Jr. and S. Smidt, *The Capital Budgeting Decision*, 2nd ed. (New York: Macmillan Co., 1966), pt. 3. For a brief discussion of the relationship between risk and the discount rate, see: Hirshleifer, DeHaven, and Milliman, *Water Supply*, pp. 139 ff.

23. There is considerable commonality between these risk aversion extremes and those implicit in situations which utilize MINIMAX and MAXIMAX objective functions for probabilistic decision-making. For an introduction to this subject, see: M. Wohl and B.V. Martin, "Evaluation of Mutually Exclusive Design Projects," *Highway Research Board Special Report*, Washington, D.C., 1966, sec. 8.3.

24. For coverage of other aspects of this subject, see Hufschmidt et al., *Criteria*, pp. 34 ff.

25. On this matter, though, with respect to water resource investments, Hirshleifer, DeHaven, and Milliman, *Water Supply*, say rather bluntly: "It is of course no secret that federal agencies, at any rate, have had a notorious history of overoptimism even on factual matters relating to prospective costs and benefits, quite aside from their conceptual errors which double-count or otherwise inflate their optimistic estimates;" pp. 145 and see also 161.

26. Hirshleifer, DeHaven, and Milliman, *Water Supply*, p. 143.

27. In addition to the remarks and references to follow, see the treatment of this subject by McKean, *Systems Analysis*, pp. 163 ff.

28. Hirshleifer, DeHaven, and Milliman, *Water Supply*, p. 146. See also their additional comments on pp. 144-48.

29. Ibid., p. 147.

30. Ibid., p. 161.

31. Hufschmidt, et al., *Criteria*, p. 67.

Chapter 3
Demand Functions, Travel Benefits, and Travel Forecasting

1. This assumption is hardly unique, and is virtually identical with a similar but implicit assumption embodied in the analyses made by Beckmann et al., Vickrey, and Walters, among others.

2. For various analytical techniques for handling the problems of modal and intratemporal demand cross-elasticities, and for determining workable demand

functions from empirical data, see: "Demand for Intercity Passenger Travel in the Washington-Boston Corridor," Systems Analysis and Research Corporation, a report to the U.S. Department of Commerce, 1963, Chapter 5; M. Wohl, "Development of Travel Forecasting Models for Trans-Bay Movement: A First Approximation," Informal Report to California State Division of Bay Toll Crossings, June 1966. Symbolically, the demand between zones i and j during hour 1 by mode 1, or $q_{ij}^{1,1}$, is:

$$q_{ij}^{1,1} = f(p_{ij}^{1,1}, p_{ij}^{2,1}, \ldots, p_{ij}^{h,1}, p_{ij}^{1,2}, p_{ij}^{2,2}, \ldots, p_{ij}^{h,2}, \ldots, p_{ij}^{h,m}),$$

where h is the number of demand periods, m is the number of modes, and $p_{ij}^{x,y}$ is the travel price for trips between zones i and j by mode y during the xth demand period.

3. The effect of income level on passengers per car for work trips is marked, and indicates that peak hour demand functions should be dimensioned by income level; for data on this aspect and on trip purpose see, for example, W. Smith and Associates, *Future Highways and Urban Growth* (Automobile Manufacturers Association, 1961), pp. 84-86.

4. See, for example, the illustrative case shown in C.H. Oglesby and L.I. Hewes, *Highway Engineering*, 2nd ed. (New York: Wiley, 1963), p. 90.

5. In other words, we will ignore the fact that demand during hour h is not only a function of the price of travel during hour h, but is also a function of the price of travel during all other hours of the day, and vice versa. (Do not confuse demand with equilibrium flow.) However, a much more complete example, which deals mathematically with the fact that demand during hour h is also a function of the price and demand for travel during *all other* hours of the day, is provided in M. Wohl, "A Methodology for Forecasting Peak and Off-Peak Travel Volumes," *Highway Research Record* No. 322, NAS-NRC (1970), pp. 208-14 (Case 2), hereinafter cited Wohl, 1970.

6. For specific details on the derivation of the price-volume and demand functions, as well as fixed roadway costs, see: M. Wohl, "The Short-Run Congestion Cost and Pricing Dilemma," *Traffic Quarterly* (January 1965), and M. Wohl, "Determination of Peak and Off-Peak Costs, Prices and Demands Under Certain Pricing Conditions and Facility Cost Allocation Methods," Discussion Paper No. 26, *Transport Research Program*, Harvard University (August 1965).

Chapter 4
Economic Efficiency, Utilization, Pricing, and Investment: The Theoretical Basis

1. An excellent and thorough discussion of the rationale underlying the requirement of equal prices to all tripmakers may be found in: J. Hirshleifer, J.C. DeHaven, and J.W. Milliman, *Water Supply: Economics, Technology and*

Policy (Chicago: The University of Chicago Press, 1960), pp. 37-40 and chap. 5.

2. However, should the facility capacity be regarded as fixed for all time, *regardless* of the expansion possibilities and consequences, and should the distributional questions loom important (which they clearly do), a more ambiguous situation develops. See: M. Wohl, "The Short-Run Congestion Cost and Pricing Dilemma," *Traffic Quarterly* (January 1966).

3. For a straightforward and more thorough treatment of this subject, see Hirshleifer, DeHaven, and Milliman, *Water Supply*, pp. 90 ff.

4. This conclusion follows from the so-called "General Theory of Second Best;" for a short and simplified discussion, see: J.R. Meyer et al., *The Urban Transportation Problem* (Cambridge: Harvard University Press, 1965), chap. 13. For a more complete discussion, see: R.K. Lancaster and R.G. Lipsey, "The General Theory of Second Best," *Review of Economic Studies*, 24 (1956-57), pp. 11-32.

5. This case has been described in some detail by A.A. Walters, "The Theory and Measurement of Private and Social Cost of Highway Congestion," *Econometrica*, 29 4 (October 1961), pp. 678-81; see also, B. Johnson, "On the Economics of Road Congestion," *Econometrica* (January-April 1964), pp. 137-50. Also, attention in this section will mainly be limited to short-run conditions.

6. See, among other references: E. Solomon, "The Arithmetic of Capital-Budgeting Decisions," and J.H. Lorie and L.J. Savage, "Three Problems in Rationing Capital," both articles in *The Management of Corporate Capital*, The Free Press of Glencoe, New York (1964), E. Solomon, ed; H. Bierman and S. Smidt, *The Capital Budgeting Decision* (New York: Macmillan Co., 1966), chap. 3; Hirshleifer, DeHaven, and Milliman, *Water Supply*, chaps. 6 and 7; M. Wohl and B.V. Martin, "Evaluation of Mutually Exclusive Design Projects," *Highway Research Board Special Report 92*, Washington, D.C., 1966, chap. 2.

7. M. Boiteux, "Peak-Load Pricing," translated by H.W. Izzard, *Journal of Business*, 33, 2,© University of Chicago Press (April 1960), pp. 157-79; this work is also included in *Marginal Cost Pricing in Practice*, edited by J.R. Nelson (New Jersey: Prentice-Hall, 1964). It should be noted that some of his mathematical results may appear different from those formulated herein, since the output time interval used by Boiteux was 12 hours; further, it may be helpful to note that Boiteux uses the term "development cost" in place of long-run marginal cost, and "differential cost" in place of short-run marginal cost. Finally, he applied the term "plant of flexible capacity" to facilities having characteristics of the sort discussed here.

8. Ibid., pp. 169 and 177-78.

9. Ibid., p. 169; notation and time-scale has been changed to conform to that used herein. The Boiteux solution can also be applied to situations with more than two different (intratemporal) demand functions.

10. Ibid., pp. 169-70.

11. Among others, Vickrey has undertaken extensive analysis of the peak-load pricing problem and has developed a slightly different approach for the determination of the differential tolls for peak and off-peak hours. See: W.S. Vickrey, "Pricing as a Tool in Coordination of Local Transportation," *Transportation Economics*, National Bureau of Economic Research, Columbia University Press (1965), pp. 284-85.

12. To examine the complications introduced by accounting for hour-to-hour demand cross-relations, see: M. Wohl, 1970.

Chapter 5
Investment Planning and Pricing in Practice

1. For a more complete treatment of this subject, see: M. Wohl, "Congestion Toll Pricing for Public Transport Facilities," *Highway Research Record* No. 314 (NAS-NRC), (1970).

2. For a fairly complete review of the alternatives, see: *Road Pricing: The Economic and Technical Possibilities*, Ministry of Transport, London (1963).

3. M. Boiteux, "Peak-Load Pricing," translated by H.W. Izzard, *Journal of Business*, 33, 2,© University of Chicago Press (April 1960), p. 166.

4. This recommendation appears to be consistent with the view of I.M.D. Little (which was adopted on somewhat different grounds, however); his discussion of consumers' surplus provides an important addendum. See: I.M.D. Little, *A Critique of Welfare Economics*, 2nd ed., Oxford University Press (1958), chap. 10. Regarding doubts among economists about the existence and measurement of upper regions of demand functions, see: J. Meyer and D. Shimshoni, "Evaluation of Benefits in Dollar Terms: The Economic Theory," from *A Method of Air Traffic Control Improvement and Application to All-Weather Landing Systems*, United Research, Inc. (1959).

5. E.F. Renshaw, "A Note on the Measurement of the Benefits from Public Investment in Navigation Projects," *The American Economic Review*, **47**, 5 (September 1957), p. 653.

6. This view seems to be commonly held by transport economists. See, for example: H. Mohring and M. Harivitz, *Highway Benefits—An Analytical Framework*, Northwestern University Press (1962), p. 38-39; also, R. Zettel, "Highway Benefits and the Cost Allocation Problem," A.A.S.H.O. Proceedings, 43rd Annual Meeting (1957).

7. It is worth noting, in this regard, that actions of this sort can create additional costs unnecessarily. As a pertinent example, consider the recent Federal legislation which will force *all* new automobiles to be equipped with pollution controls to meet arbitrary (and fixed) standards, *regardless* of the locale, costs, or purposes for which they are to be used. Since automobile air

pollution of sufficient amount to be above "tolerable" limits is confined to relatively few cities, and since virtually all the travel within these areas is made by the local residents, it is easy to argue that a nationwide solution of this sort will tend to be quite inefficient. (Former California legislation applying to *used* cars provided a more reasonable model, in that smog inhibitors had to be installed on used cars only within certain dense or critical counties within the state.) For a fairly thorough and reasonable review of these matters, see: "Cumulative Regulatory Effects on the Cost of Automotive Transportation" (RECAT), *Report to Executive Office of Science and Technology*, Washington, D.C. (February 1972).

8. See J.R. Meyer et al., *The Urban Transportation Problem* (Cambridge: Harvard University Press, 1965), pp. 60ff.

9. Ibid., chaps. 4, 8, 9, and 13. See, also: H. Mohring, "Relation between Optimum Congestion Tolls and Present Highway User Charges," *Highway Research Record* No. 47, Washington, D.C. (1964).

10. For an elaboration on these techniques, see: articles by T. Deen et al. and by M. Wohl, in *Travel Forecasting*, Highway Research Board Record No. 38, Washington, D.C. (1963); M. Beckmann et al., *Studies in the Economics of Transportation* (New Haven, Conn.: Yale University Press, 1956), chaps. 3, 4, and 5; and Wohl, 1970.

11. For a discussion of the problems involving other time interval lengths, see: M. Wohl, "Notes on Transient Queuing Behavior, Capacity Restraint Functions and their Relationship to Travel Forecasting," *Papers of the Regional Science Association,* **21** (1968).

12. See, for example: G.P. St. Clair and N. Lieder, "Evaluation of Unit Cost of Time and Strain-and-Discomfort Cost of Non-Uniform Driving," *Highway Research Board Special Report* 56, Washington, D.C. (1960).

Appendix 2
Demand Functions to Account for Intratemporal and
Intermodal Relations and Cross Relations: A First
Approximation

1. See, for example, the findings of Oi and Shuldiner with respect to local transportation and automobile expenditures; W. Oi and P. Shuldiner, *An Analysis of Urban Travel Demands* (Illinois: Northwestern University Press, 1962), chap. 6.

2. "Demand for Intercity Passenger Travel in the Washington-Boston Corridor," by *Systems Analysis and Research Corporation*, for the U.S. Department of Commerce (1963), chap. 5.

Index

Air pollution, problems from air transport, 115; costs, 25
Assumptions, basic, 3–4, 64
Automobiles: battery operated, 106n; electric, 106n

Backward-bending, 81 ff, 14n
Beckmann, M., 145–146, 148, 152
Benefit: incidence of, 114; increments of, 91 ff; distinguished from user cost, 39
Benefit conditions, 47
Benefit measurement, 125
Benefit-cost analysis, 124
Benefits: 125; daily total net, 96; external, problems of, 114; future, 90; marginal, 87; maximum total, 74; potential vs. actual, 67; surplus over costs, 97; travelers' expectations of, 2; vs. costs, 114
Berkeley, Cal., highway, 116n
Bierman, H., Jr., 148, 150
Boelter, L. M. K., xv
Boiteux, M., 98, 112, 150, 151
Boston-Washington Corridor, 126, 137
Bottleneck: see Backward bending
Bureau of the Budget, 32, 35

Capacity reductions, 83–84
Capital outlays, conversion of, 54n
Capital recovery future, 29
Car pooling, 37n, 120
Compensation, conditions for determining, 114n; to disbenefited, 116
Consumer's surplus, 40
Convergence, cobweb type of, 44
Constant returns to scale, defined, 21; 98n
Cost: functions of, 11 ff; 119, 123; incidence of, 114; incremental, 114
Costs: and benefits, 125; collection of, 106; exclusion of certain, 63; fixed, 14; future, 90; in personal resources, 2; nonhomogeneous, 117; reduction of, 133; short-run average variable, 98; variable, 85; surpassing benefits, 115; vs. benefits, 114
Council of Economic Advisers, 35
Criteria of economic welfare, 126
Cross-elasticities, 90n, 111n, 119, 120, 121

Data processing, 124–125
Decreasing returns to scale, 21n, 80, 96n, 112
Deen, T., 152

Design, elements of, of highways, 20
DeHaven, J. C., 145, 147–150
Demand, elasticity of, 49n
Demand curve for tripmaking, 37–39
Demand fluctuations, 87 ff
Demand functions, 37, 119, 120, 123; determination of, 51 ff; shift in, 47
Demand model, intercity passenger demand, 137
Discount rate, 30 ff; 34
Diseconomies, definition of, 24n
Dorfman, R., 146
Doyle Report, 145

Eckstein, O., 32, 148
Economics of transportation, 3
Effects, negative, of engineering highways, 115
Efficiency vs. fluctuations, 95
Elasticity: 129, 133, 135–137
Elements, toxic, from automobiles, 116
Engineer, role of, 2–3
Equilabration, 117
Equilibrium conditions, 124; flow, 41, 43 ff
Expenditures, increments of, 91 ff
Expansion of services, 80
External costs: see Diseconomies and Externalities
Externalities: costs to nontravelers, 115; effects on pollution, noise, damage, cost of land, involuntary displacement, personal injury, loss of life, 114; measurement of, 124; necessary, 114; neglect of, in planning, 25; user payments for, 116
"Evaluation of Free Transit Service," 137

Federal capital, social cost of, 32
Feasibility, 6, 7; financial, 10, 89, 93, 98, 101, 104n, 123
Financing of plans, 6, 8
Fixed costs, 89n
Fixed facility costs, 26
Fixed vehicle costs, 27
Flow conditions, capacity reducing, 81
Flow pattern, fluctuations in, 28; see also Fluctuations
Flow rates, equalization of, 108n
Fluctuations: demand, 87 101, 110; intertemporal, 88; and intratemporal, 63, 95
Forecasting, travel, 125
Friedman, F., 146

About the Author

Martin Wohl recently joined Carnegie-Mellon University as Professor of Transportation System Planning. Previously, he served as Director of Transportation Studies at the Urban Institute; as Manager of the Transportation Analysis Department at Ford Motor Company; as a Senior Staff member at the Rand Corporation; as a faculty member of M.I.T., Harvard University, and University of California (Berkeley); and as a consultant in various capacities. His S.B. and S.M. degrees were received from M.I.T., and his D. Eng. from University of California (Berkeley). Among many other publications, he coauthored *The Urban Transportation Problem* with John Meyer and John Kain and *Traffic System Analysis for Engineers and Planners* with Brian Martin.